Once Upon a Time in RIMC

Once Upon a Time in RIMC

A Thrilling Account of the Happy Days at the RASHTRIYA INDIAN MILITARY COLLEGE, Dehradun, from 1962 to 1966.

BRIG JASBIR SINGH, SM

OCCAM

Title: Once Upon a Time in RIMC
Author: Brig Jasbir Singh
ISBN: 978-81-949547-2-9
Edition: I

Published by:
Mugdha Misri Chakravartty for
BluOne India LLP

Publisher's Address:
306, Tower-I, Assotech Business Cresterra,
Plot No. 22, Sector 135, Noida.

Website: www.bluone.ink
Email: publisher@bluone.ink

Printed at Thomson Press (India) Ltd.

OCCAM

CONTENTS

Author's Note

I remember very well of the time a few years back when I recollected our many mischievous acts in school and wrote articles about those exciting times. However, the articles were then stashed away to be used for the proverbial rainy day. Today, as we hurtle towards the Centenary of RIMC in 2022, I feel the time has come to publish the articles. I would like to thank Unni G Kartha, my coursemate from Ranjit Section, RIMC, who has always applied his magical skills to make my articles come alive.

This book is dedicated to the long-awaited Centenary Celebrations of RIMC in 2022.

Brig Jasbir Singh, SM
Three Feathers Farm
District Nainital, Uttarakhand.

Glorious Days at RIMC

The sun had set in Dehradun (UP), and the night sky was heavily overcast with monsoon clouds. Violent flashes of lightning streaked across the darkened sky, followed by the angry rumblings of thunder. It was not a night to be far from a dry and warm bed. Soon the rain came down in sheets, accompanied by brilliant flashes of lightning and the deafening roar of thunder. It was the month of August 1962, and a new school term was to begin after a couple of days at the forty-year-old Rashtriya Indian Military College (RIMC). It was also known as *Rajwara Camp*, where young Indian princes of yesteryears had resided and trained from 1902-1922. In 1922, a school was inaugurated on the large 120-acre campus by the Prince of Wales (later King Edward VIII/Duke of Windsor). The school was called Prince of Wales Royal Indian Military College (PWRIMC) and later Royal Indian Military College (RIMC). After India's Independence in 1947 and to date, the school is called Rashtriya Indian Military College (RIMC).

My parents had accompanied me to Dehradun by train. On our arrival in the evening, we checked into the Retiring Room at the Dehradun Railway Station. I had received my 'call up' letters from Doon School where I had been registered for admission at birth in 1951, as well as from RIMC, Dehradun, where I was one of two boys who had been approved for selection from UP State. The other boy selected for admission from UP State was Cadet (later Colonel and Principal of RIMC) Arun Mamgain. Early the next morning, there was a discussion among my parents about my future – would I be joining Doon School or RIMC? My father then explained that his cousin, Pritam Singh, had joined RIMC in the 1920s, but had been poisoned to death during his vacations from school. The sad event had taken place due to some misplaced inter-family rivalry and my father wanted me to join RIMC and complete my schooling there as Pritam would have possibly done. Interestingly, my father had his way and soon we were seated in a monstrosity of a taxi cab and heading for Rajawara Camp, as the middle-aged and heavily mustachioed cab driver had called RIMC.

We drove into an old gate and entered the RIMC Estate. Then we went along the winding road to the RIMC Office that was located in a picturesque building with a sloping roof and pretty doors and windows. At the Office, we were

The author as a first-term cadet in RIMC – August 1962

met by the Duty Master and made to fill some forms. I was told that my School Number was 334, my Kit Number was 181 and I was to be in Pratap Section. The Section Master of Pratap Section was Mr. RC Singhal and the cadets wore a yellow lanyard with their olive green (OG) uniform. The Section had been known as Rawlinson Section before Independence of India in 1947. It later transpired that there were two other cadets of my name – Jasbir Singh (Dara) and Jasbir Singh Narwal – so I was called Jasbir Singh III! However, to avoid any mix-ups because of our common names, after a few days, I was transferred to Ranjit Section where Mr. GS Bisht was the Section Master and the cadets wore red lanyards with their uniforms.

After completing the paperwork and filling up some forms at the School Office we went to Holding Section where all new cadets were to be housed for the first term. Once we got to Holding Section, I removed my black metal trunk from the taxicab and placed it in the locker room. I was introduced to Cadet Ranbir Singh Ranawat, (Shivaji Section), who was an NCO and the Dormitory Commander (Dorm Com) of the Holding Section. My mother carefully emptied my trunk and neatly placed my clothes and toilet items in a small cupboard, while my father advised me on my conduct in the school. Soon it was time for parents to leave. We said our goodbyes and their taxicab left. I sat down on my wooden locker and looked around me. There were some other new cadets and their parents and guardians in the dormitory. I went and made friends with the other new cadets. It would be a long association, and as I look back today it seems like just the other day! We were impressed by our Dorm Com, who was a smart and decent soul. Ranawat would place a lock on a cupboard, insert a key and then fire an air gun pellet through the small hole.

The new cadets slept fitfully, covered with warm, red-coloured school blankets, in the newly constructed Holding Section building block. For most of these young boys, it was their first night away from the cozy, cocoons of their homes. Interesting incidents and hilarious stories of the incredible days in RIMC form a part of this book. Like all other public schools in hill stations or semi-hill stations, RIMC too has its share of sizzling ghost stories, some of which are narrated in the book.

Group of RIMC Cadets with Sardar Swaran Singh (Foreign Minister) - 1966

Standing: (L to R) Cadets DS (Fatty) Grewal, AC (Bunty) Katoch, Anil Bhalla, MMH Zaki, MP (Dada Sult) Malik, SS Thakar, Dr. Swaran Singh, Jasbir Singh (Author), Sumer Singh, Mr. SP Sharma (Principal), Swapan Bhadra, AS Kajla. Sitting: (L to R) BM Pillay, TJ Lal, AK Das, UG Kartha, Ravi Pillai, CS Lehl, Mehta, Bhanwar Singh

Ethos of a Rimcollian

At the very outset before tackling this important issue about the ethos of a *Rimcollian*, I will touch upon the basic question of who are *Rimcollians*? Very simply they are a unique breed of individuals who have been educated and trained in the unique institution called RIMC (Rashtriya Indian Military College). RIMC has also been called by various other names over the years and is located at Dehradun (North India). RIMC was inaugurated by Prince of Wales (later King Edward VIII of UK / Duke of Windsor) on 13 March 1922. Later, in 1944, in addition to the three Sections of Roberts, Kitchener, and Cornwallis, another Section, named Wavell Section, was opened for the British boys whose fathers were stationed in India. Therefore, we find *Rimcollians* in India, Pakistan, and even in the UK. Today, *Rimcollians* and their families can also be found in many countries across the world, where they have dropped anchor and settled down. I have tried to identify the unique qualities which distinguish *Rimcollians* from their colleagues, in day-to-day life. Using my own experience and that of my close friends, I have tried to learn about the unique qualities, and how and where they are generally imbibed by the cadets of RIMC.

For nearly a century, *Rimcollians* have done the three Services proud. Many *Rimcollians* who have not joined the Services, have successfully embellished the grand portals in civvy street, such as business, industry, administrative services, etc., and done very well indeed! They have proved that the alma mater trains boys who are very successful in both the Services and other vistas. All *Rimcollians* have been trained at RIMC from the tender age of eleven or twelve years. Due to their unique training and upbringing, most *Rimcollians* possess a different set of mannerisms and the sterling qualities of moral courage, truthfulness, uprightness, and a strong spirit of adventure and endurance. Most remarkable is the spirit that defies defeat! Added to these qualities is a strong sense of nationalism and the spirit to never accept defeat or give up without a jolly good fight. *Rimcollians* never fear to risk their all and will rise up to fight wholeheartedly for a rightful cause.

As young boys, we were repeatedly told that a healthy body and mind was what everyone expected of us as cadets in the school. Camaraderie and *esprit-de-corps* are two qualities we were expected to imbibe as the true benchmark of our character. A sneak, a whistle-blower, or one who reported on mischievous activities of colleagues, was deemed a despicable person and boycotted by one and all. Mischief was an essential part of our growing up process, and our indulgence could never be deterred by any form of punishment, even a caning in the Principal's office! '*Learn to be smart,*' we were told, '*Don't ever get caught!*' The solemn dictum for us to follow was '*A smart Rimcollian is never caught!*'

In our time in RIMC, no one was particular about academic brilliance on our part. They were quite happy if we did not get into any serious trouble in school and managed to get the required 40% pass-marks in our examinations. Though an average of 40% marks in examinations was considered to be adequate, our parents and teachers repeatedly sounded us to achieve a happy mix of excellence in both education and sports. Passing in the NDA Examination was mandatory, and a failure thereof was absolutely unthinkable. This mandatory requirement gave us many a sleepless night! However, it was often said there were some stalwarts who simply placed a copy of the Master-Guide* under their pillow and had a deep slumber. They hoped that adequate knowledge would surely pass from the Master-Guide to their empty heads!

Life in the armed forces was our future. It was the only choice we had at the time! Looking back, I recollect we had an incredible amount of academic pursuits which we happily took in our stride, without facing undue tensions of mugging up from our books and reproducing that knowledge during examinations. It was considered adequate if we could imbibe the basic essence of academics, pass during our examinations and move on. The RIMC curriculum had been structured for us to enter National Defence Academy (NDA), Khadakvasla, and perform well during our three-year-long training at that premier institution.

Rimcollians are generally known to be men who lead others from the front, especially when the going gets tough. They are never supposed to be browbeaten or physically suppressed by anything or anyone. On the other hand, *Rimcollians* are never expected to take up cudgels for issues that are seen to be wrong! It was repeatedly drilled into us that we should never accept defeat, but force the other party or enemy to succumb instead. Looking back today, I feel it was this quality which called on cadets to always think of defeating our colleagues from other sections! But, if we jointly felt threatened or perceived a threat to the institution of RIMC, we would rally together, drop all our differences, and jointly face a common threat. Worth seeing was our aggressive attitude during sports matches with other schools or during Doon Athletics at Doon School. We would invariably cheer remorselessly, till we were literally hoarse!

All along, we knew our lives were ultimately meant to either lead a bayonet charge with 'bolt action 303 rifles', sail in leaky ships, or fly rickety aeroplanes! So, it was courage, determination, tenacity, and resilience we needed the most, not academic brilliance! Another quality very close to the heart was moral courage. It was a matter of great pride to be honest, and this quality was highly appreciated. We would willingly own up to any wrong-doings that had either not succeeded as we had planned, or where we had been caught doing mischief! The degree of difficulty or the time of day or night for the mischief hardly mattered as long as our task was accomplished. We knew that the final accomplishment of the task would go a long way to distinguish *Rimcollians* from all the others. Today, I can state with a fair degree of surety that even during heavy combat operations, these qualities have helped *Rimcollians* overcome all adversity with a smile, and finally attain victory in battle! The courageous and magnificent actions by Capt (later Lt Gen) PS Bhagat, VC (the first Indian to win a VC in World War II), Maj Somnath Sharma, PVC (the first Indian to win a PVC), and many other *Rimcollians*, are true examples of such gallant accomplishments. There are also examples galore of *Rimcollians* who have faced extreme adversities with a smile, both in the Armed Forces and other professions. These qualities also highlight the great spirit of never accepting defeat or yielding to any adversary!

As cadets in RIMC, we often confronted one another over seemingly petty issues. These confrontations led to many a physical fight. However, these physical contests helped us to hone our skills to fearlessly tackle any sort of opposition, including that from the enemy. Honestly, I feel the finest quality we learnt, was how to tackle adversity with a smile on our faces! Whether it was a simple inter-section boxing match, a heated fist-fight in school, or combat in battle, the smile remained pasted on our faces and it would shock our adversaries. The smile gave immense confidence to us and made it much easier to gain victory. Interestingly, in RIMC all our petty animosities were quickly forgotten, and these confrontations led to priceless, lifelong friendships. Nowadays, there has been a lot of change and the battles are more often fought in boardrooms and backrooms rather than the classic battlefield. But the qualities required to achieve success or victory are nearly always the same. These priceless qualities have been gained by *Rimcollians* in the playing fields of RIMC and these 'old boys' hold the key through the many mischievous activities they have been a part of. However, present-day perceptions have changed and there is no doubt that one has to study with equal zest as one does while playing games. This is because the brain is as important as brawn. Thus, there has to be a slight shift of focus to allow cadets to embrace the present trends.

The boys who have been trained in RIMC shall forever be members of a very select band of individuals, who are called *Rimcollians*. Over the years, these *Rimcollians* who have passed out from the hallowed portals of RIMC, gradually begin to display the awesome qualities which they have imbibed in the college. As these *Rimcollians* weather life, they mature into very humble and distinguished personalities, in the Services, civilian walks of life, or wherever they may be. In the final analysis, *Rimcollians* are the valuable product of a unique institution in Dehradun, called RIMC. In later life, what separates the *Rimcollians* from all the others, is their gracious humility and a host of sterling qualities. These qualities have been imbibed during the 'rough and tumble' of times spent at the playfields of RIMC. It would be unbecoming of me not to mention this great quality of never giving up when involved in a fight! Lastly, it is overly asserted that the great qualities possessed by *Rimcollians* are in no small measure due to the simple-minded mischief they have been involved in at some point of time during their stay in RIMC.

The 'Side Pike' Dive

This particular story splashes through various swimming pools at New Delhi, Lucknow, and Ambala Cantt, before reaching the 'Old Swimming Pool' at RIMC, Dehradun. I will start from the crowded pool at the National Sports Club of India (NSCI), New Delhi. In 1960, I was spending my summer holidays in New Delhi, while studying in La Martinere College, Lucknow (two years before I had joined RIMC, Dehradun). Since it was warm, I would go for a swim each morning and afternoon.

One day as I was merrily doing the 'Non-Swimmer's Dog Paddle' at the pool's shallow end when all of a sudden I was violently pushed underwater with considerable force and violence. I sputtered noisily to the surface and lashed out wildly with my arms. My feet quickly touched the bottom and I stood erect in the knee-deep water. I looked around me and discovered that a very fat man had jumped on me and now he was busy splashing his hands and blowing like a beached whale!

'*He must be a non-swimmer like me,*' I said to myself as I pushed myself towards him.

'*Very sorry,*' he said with a genial smile, '*I tripped and fell on you. I hope you aren't hurt?*'

Gallantly I shook my head to convey I was okay. Looking up at the clouded sky I couldn't make out the Sun's position to know the time of day. Thus, I genuinely asked the fat man, '*Sir, please tell me if it is morning or afternoon?*'

He gave me a very surprised look and must have thought I'd gone mad. He looked at me and asked me again very seriously, '*I hope you are okay, young man*?'

As the hot days went by, he became a swimming-pool-friend, and we both gradually learnt our basic swimming and succeeded in doing a complete breadth of the pool without putting our feet down on the floor.

When vacations were over, I returned to my school at Lucknow. I was proud of my swimming achievements and told all my friends with appropriate exaggerations. I never knew that the Inter-House Swimming Competition was upon us and our House (Cornwallis House) was looking desperately for a swimmer to participate in Junior Freestyle Relay. Some seniors asked me if I knew how to do freestyle. Proudly, I replied in the affirmative, and lo and behold, I was promptly informed I had been selected for the swimming team! My joy knew no ends and since there was no time for practice sessions, it transpired I would take my inaugural plunge during the competition itself!

The big day arrived, and there I was standing at the deep end of the pool. I was the second swimmer of my team in the Junior Freestyle Relay Race and wore a fancy-looking, cobalt-blue coloured swimming trunks, which I had borrowed from a kindly friend.

There was an incessant roar of loud cheering from the excited audience. The loud sound reverberated within the confines of our enclosed swimming pool. The race began and the first swimmer of our House was in the lead, as he swam in freestyle to the pool's end where I was standing.

As he touched the pool's end, a senior boy standing at my side slapped my shoulder and said loudly above sounds of the loud cheering, '*GO!*'

Without another thought, I leapt into the water like a crab and landed with a big splash. Even though I madly flailed my arms and legs amidst the loud roar of cheering, I knew I was not moving forward. I felt myself slowly sinking. Desperately, I thought of my great achievements at the NSCI Pool and even of my 'fat friend' in New Delhi. But, it was to no avail and I kept on sinking! With desperate efforts to regain the surface, I must have opened my mouth to suck in badly needed air. But, instead of sweet air I took in deep gulps of freshly chlorinated water and sank even lower. As my rapidly flailing feet did not touch the pool's deep-end floor, I seriously panicked and thought I was going to drown and die! However, I suddenly felt a sharp poke on my back. I immediately reached back and took hold of a long bamboo stick that had been lowered to save me from drowning. Unceremoniously, I was pulled out of the water and quickly jerked to the safety of the cement poolside.

I was retching loudly and making unearthly sounds as I threw out the large amounts of water I had consumed. To add to my discomfiture, as I was being pulled to safety with the bamboo pole, suddenly, I spied something familiar and saw a cloth that was cobalt blue in colour. I instantly realised with intense horror that the cobalt-blue-coloured floating object was my borrowed swimming trunks! The swimming trunks had slid off my body when I had been pulled up with the long bamboo pole. On seeing my undressed state, initially, loud catcalls filled the swimming pool. Then, on seeing my sad state suddenly the wild yelling abruptly ceased and there was a hushed silence in the pool.

My eyes met the horrified gaze of our House Swimming Captain, who was desperately mouthing something and gesturing to his swimming trunks. While I was still in the water, I grabbed my floating swimming trunks and pulled them on. Our relay team was disqualified, and we were roundly booed by all the students. If looks could kill, I should surely have been a very dead swimmer from Cornwallis House, La Martinere College!

In 1962, I moved to Ambala Cantt. In August of that year, I joined RIMC, Dehradun. Before moving to Dehradun, I again made a few visits to a swimming pool located in the Army area. Here, some young officers (YOs) of 13 Kumaon took me under their tutelage and began to teach me to dive. They took me up the five metres high fixed diving board and proceeded to give me lessons in diving from that height. I was also taught to execute the plain dive from the one metre high springboard.

After the unsavoury fiasco during the Inter-House Swimming Competition at La Martinere College, Lucknow, I had stayed away from all swimming races, and concentrated instead, on learning to dive.

Later, in RIMC, I volunteered for diving and floating events. I was turned away from the floating event as there was a stream of shammers waiting to take part in that easy event. I found a vacant slot to participate in the diving event for Ranjit Section Swimming Team. We began practice sessions and I was asked to indicate the types of dives I could execute. I said I would execute the 'plain dive' from both upper and lower diving boards. The Ranjit Section Swimming Captain patiently told me that the 'plain dive' (as I had called it), was actually known as the 'English Header'. But I could not perform only the 'English Header', as it was a simple dive and had the lowest performance value. I found our Swimming Captain to be extremely knowledgeable. Since the YOs of 13 Kumaon at Ambala Cantt had taught me only the simplest dive, I quickly began to master other types of dives as well.

I saw the other diver of our section team bounce up from the springboard and perform a difficult dive. He would become airborne, bend himself in mid-air and touch his toes. He would then, straighten out in the air with his toes held together and pointing upwards and gently enter the water.

The Section Swimming Captain ambled over to me and said, '*See that difficult dive with a high performance value? It's called "Pike Dive". Now go and try it out if you can.'*

So, I mounted the diving board, ran forward for two and a half steps, jumped down hard on the diving board, and automatically rose into the air. I easily bent my body and touched my toes, while keeping my knees very straight. Then I straightened out and slipped head-first into the water. However, while I was straightening my body after touching my toes, I felt my body involuntarily twist to one side. As I splashed into the water, I thought I had spoiled the dive with my involuntary body-twist. When I came to the surface and sat at the poolside, I saw the Section Swimming Captain approach me at a half run. I was scared and wanted to slip back under the water and hide.

However, as I sat there with my eyes closed, the smiling Swimming Captain patted me on my back and said, '*By God, Jasbir you are a bloody natural! That was a beautiful "Side Pike Dive", and it has a colossal performance value. How did you do it?*'

I couldn't answer him as I didn't know myself how I could have executed a perfect 'Side Pike Dive!'

On the day of the swimming competition, I was dressed in my swimming trunks (this time I had ensured they were tightly fastened!). With my colleagues, I entered the swimming pool from the small door towards the Old Raquet Court. The floating event was about to begin, as we trooped in and went to the pool's deep end. I waited in line with other divers near the springboard. We had been asked to record the type of dives we would perform from the high diving board and springboard, on a clip-board held by Mr. HD Puri, our Cricket Coach and Art Master. I told Mr. Puri I would be doing an 'English Header' from the high board and a 'Side Pike' from the ground level springboard.

On hearing that I would do a 'Side Pike', Mr. Puri looked at me with keen interest and raised his eyebrows in mock surprise. '*I hope you know what "Side Pike Dive" is?*' he asked.

I smiled and other cadets asked me what Mr. Puri had said. I told them I would be doing a 'Side Pike', but no one knew what the dive was all about!

When the floating event was over, it was time for the diving event to begin. A shrill whistle blast was sounded and cadets maintained silence. A dapper-looking Mr. RC Sharma, in a blue blazer, grey flannel trousers with a striped tie, picked up the microphone and announced the 'Diving Event'. My name was announced and Mr. RC Sharma said I would be performing, the 'English Header' with a Tarot Value of 1.1 (*I think!*). There were claps and a few shouts of '*Come on Ranjit, Buck up Ranjit!*'.

I climbed the steps to the five metres high fixed-board and stood at its end. There was silence as I took my stance. I felt nervous as everyone in the pool seemed to be looking up at me. I quickly raised my arms to the side, brought them above my head, and took off from the diving board. I hurtled through the air with my eyes closed. The water level seemed miles away and I kept hurtling through the air. The moment I opened my eyes to see how I had yet to go, my face suddenly received a resounding slap from the water. I went underwater and quickly rose to the surface. The Swimming Pool was filled with loud cheers as the three judges (teachers) held up their slates with marks given out of 10.

After three dives from the high-diving board, we went and stood behind the ground level springboard. Once again Mr. RC Sharma announced our names and the type of dive and its performance value over the Public Address System.

When my turn came, he announced, '*Now Cadet Jasbir Singh of Ranjit Section will perform the "Side Pike" dive from the one metre springboard. Its performance value is....*'.

There was an audible gasp followed by massive cheering when cadets heard the name of the dive and its high performance value. I climbed onto the springboard and stood at attention. Loud cheers and a piercing whistle blast, followed by an announcement over the microphone, '*Silence please!*'.

There was silence followed by more cheers. Oblivious of the cheering, I took two-and-a-half steps on the springboard, jumped and rose into the air. I touched my toes, straightened out and prayed for the involuntary body turn before I entered the water. As I surfaced, I heard loud cheers and was sure that my involuntary body twist had worked. When I saw the points I had received from the three judges (7-7-6), it was confirmed that the involuntary body-twist had worked.

Gradually, the 'Side Pike Dive' became my speciality from the one metre diving board, and I came to be known as 'Diving Khalsa'. This bonanza continued during my stay in RIMC and for the three years in NDA (Kharakvasla), as well.

Phuntru's Unknown Obsession

A common predicament facing all cadets in RIMC was the poor health of our footgear – so lovingly bought from a Bata shoe shop by our parents! After intensive sessions of front-rolling and kicking of stones, our black, patent leather shoes often resembled a jaded bird's nest, with a lot of loose stitches and toothbrush-ended shoe-laces! In school, a tragedy was deemed to have struck when the front portion of the leather sole parted company with the discoloured shoe uppers and flapped resoundingly as we tried to march smartly to the mess. We were mortally scared of being checked and punished by our Section NCOs during the evening roll-call.

'*After dinner in PT kit*' was generally the dreaded announcement we heard as the NCO smugly moved down the lines of serious-looking cadets, who had fallen-in on the Parade Ground. We tried desperately to spruce up our shoes and even rubbed them with a large, red-coloured flower that was grown in the flower beds in front of the mess. We called it a shoe-flower and never got to know its common name, leave alone the botanical one[1]! We usually conducted this life-and-death exercise in pairs. While one cadet was busy rubbing the flower on his shoes, the other one would act as a 'look-out' and give early warning of an approaching *mali*. Generally, we would drop the shoe-flowers and run like mad, but if the *mali* was too close for us to break contact, we would abruptly change track, smile sweetly, and compliment him on the beautiful flowers all around us! Our reactions had been well-honed, with a lot of practice.

A short-term remedy for the flapping-sole was to untie the shoe-lace, move it under the offending sole and retie it on the uppers. However, these homemade remedies worked only for a short time and we were forced to rush urgently to Phuntru's *Mochi* Shop for emergency aid[2], before being punished during the evening fall-in. We would go to the garden (opposite the mess) before the roll-call and polish our horrible-looking shoes with hibiscus flowers, much to the annoyance of the college's gardeners.

Roll-call

The *mochi* shop was located a long way from our dormitory and behind the college *mandir*. The *mochi* would

---

1 *Much later in life, I learnt from my 'know it all' wife, that our 'shoe-flowers' were actually known as hibiscus!*

2 *Many years later, when I was attending border related talks with Chinese Govt. officials in Beijing, as Director MO-1, when I found my right shoe making a very familiar sound! Looking down, to my horror I found that my shoe sole had come loose and was flapping noisily. Initially I was nonplussed and did not know how to wriggle out of the predicament. Suddenly, the 'homemade remedies' I had learnt in RIMC came flooding back and I politely bent over and secured the shoe-sole with my lace!*

generally be seated on the floor of the small verandah in front of his one-room shop. He would squat on the floor with his legs folded under his ample behind. Phuntru would be surrounded by many pairs of ragged shoes and boots that had seen better days.

On seeing us approach the shop, he would drop his implements and clap his hands on his forehead and announce loudly to no one in particular, '*Cadet loog, ab kya chahie Phuntru se? Mera sirr khane aa gaye phir.*'

We would then be very nice to him, smile and say, '*Phuntru-ji, aaj kaisa hai haal aapka? Aapki tabiyat kaisi hai? Garmi bahut ho rahi hai!*'

He would shrug his shoulders and dismiss our efforts to please him. Out of habit, he would then look at our dis-coloured shoes, shake his head in sheer disgust and reach for a small, round, metal box and mumble, '*Mujhe pata hai tum yahan kyun aaye ho.*'

Without another word, he would pry open the lid with a hollow sound and shove down two fingers wrapped in a dirty brown cloth. The cloth would re-appear liberally smeared with a dark solution, which he would proceed to rub onto our almost white shoes. When Phuntru had finished, our shoes would be well blackened and gleam as if they were new! Later, the shoes were to be polished by us till they really shone, by using black Cherry Blossom boot polish and water. This was done before the Inspection Parade (IP). Thus, another visit to Phuntru's shop was a real necessity before the AO's IP. Our homemade remedies worked wonders and got us out of many a tight spot as we moved on with our lives.

Phuntru would be quite surprised if we did not have a flapping shoe-sole to be fixed with stitches of waxed twine. After our shoes had been blackened and we had praised him enough, Phuntru would be respectfully asked to show us his latest creations. Looking around to ensure that no one was watching him, Phuntru would reluctantly rise to his feet with loudly cracking knees. '*Band-baaja*' we would later comment and rudely laugh at the sound we had heard coming from his knees! After all these years when I hear my own knees making the '*band-baaja*' sound, I cannot help thinking of poor Phuntru and laugh quite uncontrollably. Grumbling loudly, he would go inside the small room at the back of his shop. Looking around to see that no newcomers had arrived at the shop, Phuntru would emerge with his latest coup-de-resistance. Few in college knew of Phuntru's bizarre hobby.

We had learnt of it by accident, when on one summer day we had barged into his shop unannounced, to quickly get a flapping shoe-sole repaired. That is when we discovered that in his spare time, Phuntru would finely cut the heads off the latest photographs of film actresses of the period (Vyjanthimala, Helen, Asha Parekh, Sadhna, Saira Banu etc.) and paste them onto the sexy bodies of girls that had been cut from a glossy *Playboy* magazine. The images were then hung all over the walls of the inner room of Phuntru's two-roomed *mochi* shop.

The images crafted by Phuntru were rather

incongruous with varying colours and scales. In some images, the head was much larger than the sexy body, while in others it was the other way around. We could not contain ourselves after what we had seen and burst out in uncontrollable laughter. Phuntru charged into the room when he heard our peals of loud laughter. He saw we had slyly entered the *mochi* shop and was understandably annoyed. However, after we had showered loads of praise on him, he calmed down and smiled glibly. But, he wouldn't allow us to leave until he had extracted a solemn promise that we would not tell anyone about his *art*, especially his mortal enemy, the bearded *pandit-ji* who lived in the mandir, next door to his *mochi* shop.

After that day we were good friends with Phuntru, and he ensured that our shoes were ever shining. However, I will never know if any Welhams School girls ever noticed that the three of us would have the most highly polished and gleaming shoes of all RIMC cadets who went to write our Indian School Certificate (ISC) Exams in Doon School![3]

---

[3] *Years later I sadly learnt that good old Phuntru and his entire family were washed away to their deaths in a 'flash flood', while crossing a nullah while returning from Haridwar.*

The Witch's Brew

The drop of perspiration cascaded down my forehead and splashed on the floor of the locker room, Ranjit Section, Middle Dormitory. I had formulated a homemade remedy to suffer less while undergoing punishments given by my seniors. I would switch off my mind from the punishment being undertaken and concentrate on something quite different. Having recently read a number of comic books on World War II, my mind was spiralling away in that direction. With great evil intent, I imagined I was a bomb aimer aboard a World War II bomber aircraft. I vividly imagined the aircraft was on a bombing run, and I desperately tried to direct my drops of sweat to land on an unfortunate ant, that was walking on the cement floor, below me. After the first drop of sweat plopped on the cement floor, the ant began to desperately zig-zag and take evasive action, to avoid my pseudo bombardment! The reason behind my violent intentions was directly related to the unnatural position I had been ordered to adopt. I was almost upside down, with my feet perched on a tall, wooden locker. My head hung low and my hands rested on the cool cement floor.

I was in a position that was called '*legs up and hands down*'! My recently consumed supper gurgled noisily in my stomach, and threatened to exit unceremoniously from my partly open mouth! My acrobatic position had not been adopted voluntarily and nor was I the only one ending the march day, in such an ungainly posture. Both, to my left and to my right were friends of mine, who were huffing and puffing noisily in similar bat-like postures!

The cause of our intense misery stood near us, with hands on his hips and a sardonic smile plastered on his face. He was the hyperactive, disciplinarian, dormitory NCO of Ranjit Section Middle Dorm, who had turned our existence a living hell. A few of us in the dorm could never do anything right and, therefore, we were often made to adopt the weirdest of postures, after doing rounds or front-rolls on jagged bricks that lined the central lawns, which we called the Quadrangle!

Before dinner, we had failed to accurately amplify the initials of his five-tier Malayalee name, with around 48 alphabet. My friend and classmate, Unni, another Malayalee joker with an equally long name, had told us that the NCO's name actually was an entire postal address! In Punjab, we had simple names, like 'Chunnu, Munnu, or Pappu', and if you were a girl, you could even be called 'Dollar, Pound, or Yen'. Malayalee names, however, were a mouthful which we could, unfortunately, never quite remember.

Visibly annoyed, the NCO had ordered us, '*See me after dinner in PT kit, you useless jokers!*'

So, here we were, in various lizard-like postures and adorning the Middle Dormitory Locker Room's wall, upside down like Spider-Man. Meanwhile, the NCO rubbed his hands together in utter glee, at our extreme discomfiture.

The next day was Sunday and we, the offenders of the previous night, who could not master the complicated *Malayalee Postal Addresses*, that was masquerading as the Dorm Com's name, sat on the flight of steps, before the locker room. Here, we poured out our woes to one another. We cursed our luck to have such a demonic Dorm Com, while all our other friends in Pratap and Shivaji were having a great time! It just did not seem right, and we took a solemn pledge to do something about our grave problem.

L to R: Jasbir, Kajla, Manu Dutt, Fatty Grewal, Unni Kartha
in front of Ranjit Section Middle Dorm 1964/65

But, we could not decide on what we could do, without inviting more punishment onto ourselves. So, we sat on the steps and thought in earnest, trying to find a solution to our problem.

Suddenly one of the cadets had a brain wave and said, '*Guys, Holi is just around the corner. Let's prepare a horrible mixture and rub it into his ruddy hair. That should serve him right and he'll always remember the drubbing he will get.*'

The idea to sort out the Dorm Com had our support and nodded our heads in unison. We would be able to extract our revenge, and the Dorm Com would never know the cadets who had carried out the horrible act.

As the next day was Holi, we gathered that night in the thick hedgerow behind our dormitory. We had imaginatively brought all possible ingredients for the 'witches brew' we were about to prepare. The concoction would be a mixture of incredible ingredients, like Cherry Blossom Black Boot Polish, the white polish used for PT shoes, Ponds Cold Cream, assorted hair oils, bottles of Quink Ink (blue and black), liberal squeezes of various brands of toothpaste, Fixo (the starch-like paste that HS Vaid used to pat down his fledging beard), pieces of soap of different varieties, liberal amounts of soap nut powder which we used as hair shampoo in those days, dog biscuits, leftover amounts of evening tea, and any other item we could lay our hands on.

As a late arrival, Fatty Grewal came puffing to the fire and emptied a fancy-looking bottle into our half-filled Dalda tin can. On being asked what he had added, with a conspiratorial smile Fatty held up an empty bottle whose label read Anne French Hair Remover! Fatty was a very resourceful cadet, and don't ask from where he got the stuff! It was said the bottle had been liberated from the Section Masters' house when he was summoned for counselling regarding some mischievous antics.

The old yellow-coloured can of Dalda vegetable oil with its fancy ingredients was put on three bricks that had been placed around a small fire. Just as the awful brew began to boil, there were flashes of lightening over Mussoorie, followed by deep growls of thunder.

Someone in our gatherings announced very appropriately in a croaky voice, '...*When shall we meet again? In thunder, lightning or in rain?*'

On hearing the croaky voice saying the well-timed quote from Shakespeare's *Macbeth*, we all burst out laughing. Having recently read the book in class, our surreptitious mission suddenly seemed to be very exciting and relevant.

In sheer exuberance, we wanted to yell loudly, '*Three cheers for Macbeth's Witches...*', but as secrecy and discretion were vital for our clandestine mission, we indulged in no such heroics, but rather quietly fanned the fire and performed our task of boiling the 'witch's brew'.

However, one of the cadets by the fire could not control himself and announced loudly, '*If only old Shakespeare knew what we were up to tonight, he would have done a somersault in his grave!*"

After a couple of boils, we noticed that the foul-smelling concoction had shrunk to about half its volume. It was now a lump of black, congealed mass. Once our job was completed, we stamped out the fire and carefully carried the Dalda tin into our dormitory. Due to my recent hat-trick run of 'after dinner in PT kit' punishments, I was the hero of the dorm. Thus, I had the honour to anoint our NCO's hair with our 'witch's brew'. Glad with our achievements, we carefully hid the Dalda tin containing the 'witch's brew' and dived into our beds. As thunder increased in intensity, we happily drifted into a deep slumber.

The next morning, we were up early. Dressed in our striped night suits, we excitedly opened the locker in which we had hidden the 'brew'. We had barely been able to press down the lid of the Dalda tin when our Dormitory NCO had entered the room. On seeing us huddled near the locker, he loudly asked us what we were doing.

On hearing his voice, we bleated '*Nothing, Sir*' and ran from the locker room.

The NCO yelled after us, '*You jokers today is 'Holi'. So, when we go around the college, behave yourselves and don't try anything funny or later I'll sort you fellows out, nice and proper.*'

We didn't hear anymore as we had done a skid-turn and ran out of the locker room and into the dormitory. Later, wearing our PT kit and carrying our precious Dalda tin, we joined the gang of nicely-coloured cadets who were shouting '*Holi hai*' and moving towards the

Chandragupta Section.

On the way, we were accosted by a gang of cadets from the Shivaji Section, who had been hiding behind the boilers with paper bags filled with dry coloured powder. There was great happiness and gaiety in the air as we rubbed colour onto one another. All the while I was tightly holding the precious Dalda tin. Fortunately, no one seemed to be interested in the Dalda tin.

However, one of the cadets from the Shivaji Section had asked me expectantly, '*What do you have in that Dalda tin, and why are you carrying it so carefully? Are there any sweets in it?*'

With a casual laugh, I had negated the cadet's assertions, but I had a very strong urge to open the can's lid and give him some sweets! After the brief halt at Chandragupta Section, the group became bigger and more boisterous, as a large gang of well coloured cadets joined us from Pratap Section. From Chandragupta Section we proceeded towards the swimming pool and on to the fast-flowing Garhi Nala. There was a lot of cheering and shouting that invariably ended in a loud chorus of '*Holi Hai!*'

As the group moved, we patiently kept our target in full view. At the swimming pool, some cadets of our dormitory expectantly nudged me and whispered loudly, '*We will soon reach Garhi Nala. Do it now or Holi will be over and we will have missed a great opportunity.*'

I nodded in agreement with them and moved closer to our target, who was happily dancing around in gay abandon and shouting '*Holi Hai*' in a thick Malayalee

Section looked at our smiling faces and thought we were really enjoying Holi! So, they came near us and began to clap and sing loudly.

However, a harshly whispered, '*Off with you, you miserable wretches!*' sent them, and their absurd singing, on their way to annoy some other group.

Much later, after the rowdy celebrations had ended, someone spied the Dorm Com quietly sneak into Middle Dormitory. The Dorm Com must have thought no one had seen him, but our spies were very alert. They immediately reported that a portion of the Dorm Com's scalp was seen as being devoid of any hair! Early next day, the Dorm Com visited the barber shop and shaved off all his hair with a razor. That day, we had laughed and laughed amongst ourselves, till we could barely stand. Then, with a straight face, we went up to our Dorm Com and asked him if all was well at home. He tried to deflect our questions, but we persisted and told him that a shaved head indicated that a sad event had occurred in the family. Fed up with our pseudo-concern, he kept saying all was well. Despite his frenzied splashing in Garhi Nala, followed by repeated hot water baths with sweet-smelling soaps, a faint whiff of the 'witch's brew's' terrible odour still rose to meet our noses. Thus, we abruptly cut short our concerns for the harassed NCO, and rapidly moved away to a safer area. Here, we simply thought of the Dorm Com's shaved head and laughed and laughed and laughed! It had been a highly successful pay-back time and we were happy to have extracted a terrible revenge!

accent.

When I was at an arm's length away from the D Com, I pried open the Dalda tin's lid. A foul smel mediately rose from the tin in my hand. Without delay, I scooped out a handful of the black, foul-s ing, gooey stuff and rubbed it into the Dorm Com's with a good-natured shout of '*Holi Hai*'.

Without a pause, he kept up his stupid danc even replied to my shouts, with a good-natured *Hai*'.

I felt someone yank the Dalda tin from my Throwing caution to the wind, other harassed ca Ranjit Section Middle Dorm plunged their han the tin, extracted blobs of the 'witch's brew' ar tered it all over the Dorm Com's hair and fac were nearly a dozen cadets in the fray. By now smell was unbearably overpowering.

Sensing the smelly globs of our obnoxious ' his face and hair, the Dorm Com suddenly blood-curdling scream and broke away from th cadets celebrating Holi with gay abandon. H like a demented soul and took a flying leap int ing, waist-deep waters of Garhi Nala. Some c already in the water, splashing merrily and w their colour to mark the end of the Holi festiv ately, the Dorm Com elbowed his way to th the stream and feverishly began to rub his h with the cold water. Seeing his demented face contorted with rage, we couldn't cont and began to laugh loudly. Our friends

The erstwhile Middle Dorm Commander (NCO) went on to become a very senior army officer with many achievements and accolades, but he always remained a stickler for discipline. He is now a very nice and honourable *Rimcollian* old boy, who leads a fully satisfied retired life, ensuring that his grand-child grows up like Spider Man. I guess he still says, '*Legs up, hands down*', to ensure his grand-child doesn't behave like us – the rascals of Ranjit Section Middle Dormitory, back in 1964.

Cutting Bounds

The dreaded words of Maj KC Anand, our strict Administrative Officer (commonly known as AO) rang loud and clear in our ears as we excitedly readied the private clothes we were to wear for our outing.

The previous evening, AO had got final-termers together on the cemented tennis court and threatened us with a grim, '*Listen very carefully you chaps. You'll soon be going to NDA, so watch it during your last days here in college. I'll tolerate no funny stuff like cutting bounds. If you are caught, I promise you will be sent home, right away. You can then forget about NDA and all!*'

It had been a dire threat and we well understood the importance. But our plan for the 'cutting bounds adventure' had been well-rehearsed and it was to take place on that very night. Our plans called for three of us, DS Fatty Grewal, Avtar S Kajla, and me, to hire cycles from Garhi Market and go to *Capri* Cinema Hall to see the 9 to 12 Show of *April Fool*, starring Saira Banu, etc.

During dinner, the three of us maintained an unusual silence. Our friends were quite surprised when we missed a golden opportunity to heckle our friend, DS (Dope) Chauhan, and some others, for getting us ticked off by Mr. GS Bisht, our house-master. We maintained a poker face all through the meal. After we had announced to all cadets on our table that we were coming down with some kind of flu, we were not disturbed, and nor was our peculiar silence questioned during the dinner. We were happy that after the explanation for our silence the other cadets did not pry and there was no chance for them to get even a whiff of our adventurous plans.

Fever and flu were the normal ravages that we would suffer from time to time. It was widely rumoured that the matron in the infirmary was responsible for periodically spreading the virus in the mess, so she could get her hands on more patients and thereby justify her job in the infirmary! A cruel joke really, but at the time we used to be thrilled with the humour of it all and would laugh with abandon. The actual fact, however, was that cadets would give the infirmary a wide berth because of their eternal fear of injections with long needles which the matron would remorselessly thrust into our upper arms. While she injected us, she would grind her teeth and smile with total glee. We really did not know which was worse, the injections or the matron's dreaded face?

Those were the days of colourful mixtures, pills, and the all important injections. Antibiotics were still not very popular. There are recollections of my good friend and schoolmate, UG Kartha, who remembers during an outbreak of measles in RIMC, he was admitted in the infirmary. Thus, he got to watch the matron's functioning from close quarters. She had three large glass jars filled with green, brown, and yellow coloured liquids. It was said that the matron prepared the multi-coloured concoctions on moonless nights, behind the filtration plant of our swimming pool! In the MI room, if a cadet complained of a medical problem above the chest, he was given medication from the green liquid; the brown liquid was for problems between the chest and navel, while the yellow liquid was for problems below the navel! The manner in which we were made to consume the foul-tasting liquid was itself a unique procedure. The matron would grab a conical glass container from a shelf and speedily fill it from one of the jars and hand it to the poor cadet. Seeing her contorted nose, angry frown, and beady eyes staring straight into his face, the unfortunate cadet would pinch his nose and throw the foul-smelling and equally foul-tasting liquid down his gullet. As a way of protest, a desperate body shrug was all we were permitted, before being given a chit and asked to march out of the MI Room. I am quite certain that the ingesting of the matron's foul liquids has stood all *Rimcollians* in good stead. Rarely has a *Rimcollian* lad been found wanting later in life, when made to down fiery, neat liquor during a young officer's dining-in party or on other occasions. Just a remembrance of the matron's terrifying looks and the foul smell and taste of her obnoxious liquid remedies was enough to allow for a smooth 'n' swift downing of any fiery substance that exists!

After dinner, we hurriedly changed our clothes in the large locker room of Ranjit Section Senior Dormitory. Though we were forbidden to keep private clothes and a host of other things, most of us kept a pair or so safely stashed away. We used innovative places to stash away the forbidden items, including some cash, to ensure they were not easily found by our inquisitive Masters during a surprise check-up. This very unpopular exercise was called 'Master's Raids' by the distraught cadets. The raids were deeply disliked because very often our goodies of forbidden tuck or precious money was unearthed. This was a major tragedy and serious introspection would then be done by the most devious minds available in school, to find a new hiding place for our illegal stuff!

Very soon, Kajla was nattily dressed in colourful private clothes, with a multi-coloured silk scarf around his neck. The fruity fragrance of a carefully hidden spray followed him around the Locker Room. Fatty and I felt like country bumpkins in our OG cotton trousers, terylene shirts, and PT shoes.

On our way to Garhi market, Fatty asked me seriously, '*Jas, are you carrying a bloody hanky?*'

I shook my head in the negative and said, '*No I'm not, but are you carrying the money?*'

Fatty pointed towards Kajla who nodded and slapped his pocket to assure the two of us that we were not going to be left high, and dry.

The strong, all-pervading perfume that Kajla was wearing wafted around us as we cut across the athletics ground and proceeded towards the isolated gate near the *gobar gas* plant.

'*No girls are going to be conned by your stupid perfume,*' I said to Kajla. '*You'll only end up getting us caught with this smelly stuff.*'

'*Don't you dare call this wonderful perfume names. It is anything but smelly,*' Kajla had countered, '*You guys really know nothing about what dames like! This is an expensive perfume that my brother got from Bombay!*'

Fatty raised a hand beckoning us to be quiet as we were approaching the gate. Knowing the gate to be locked, we climbed over it and were soon in Garhi market. Due to our earlier notorious, night-time exploits, Fatty seemed to intimately know the cycle shop owner. The youngish looking man had a crew cut and was draped in a *lungi*. He seemed to realise the gravity of our mission, for he asked us to quickly come inside his shop. He stood at the door, with hands on his hips and smiled like a fellow conspirator! We hired two ramshackle bicycles that looked like they had seen better days. We did not have the money to hire a third bicycle, so it was decided that Fatty would sit on the carrier of my cycle and we would swap places during the return journey. Then, Fatty was to cycle with me sitting on the carrier. For the two bicycles, Kajla paid up a princely sum of Rs 10 in advance. Only then were we permitted to wheel the cycles onto the Post Office road.

We mounted the cycles and pedalled furiously past the Army's Brigade HQ, Cambrian Hall School, Sub-Area Commander's bungalow, and Doon School. It felt great with a cool breeze fanning our faces. At the crossroads adjoining 58 GTC Officers' Mess, a Royal Enfield motorcycle passed us and went down the road towards RIMC, making a deep '*dhup, dhup, dhup*' sound from the exhaust. Seated on the motorcycle, was a thick-set man whom we could easily recognise as Mr. HD Puri[4], our Art Teacher and Cricket Coach. Quite sure he had seen three RIMC cadets on cycles, Puri must have guessed we were cutting bounds, for he swung his motorcycle around and flashed its headlight down the road. We knew we were in serious trouble if we were caught and so we pedalled like mad and put a lot of distance between us and Puri, hoping this would dissuade him from following us.

We had just passed the Doon School gate when we came upon two drunks staggering in the middle of the road. One of them was taking swigs from a half-filled bottle.

As they weaved their way from side to side, Kajla rapidly sounded his cycle bell and also yelled loudly, '*Drunks*!'

To me, it sounded like the '*Land Ahoy*!' call from the 'crow's nest' of a sailing ship.

Scenes from the *Count of Monte Cristo*[5] flashed

---

[4] *Mr. HD Puri was commonly called 'Halwa Dahin Puri' by the cadets. He was known to be a 'stickler', who would rarely give up, after he had spied RIMC cadets cutting bounds*

[5] *'Count of Monte Cristo' by Alexander Dumas had been our English textbook and we had enjoyed many a wonderful days in class, reading the book and enacting the story under the tutelage of Mr. Dunwell, Master from a school in UK. He was in India, under the Teachers Exchange Program. Dunwell would often play his trumpet and entertain us in class, much to the annoyance of Mr. SP Sharma, our Principal. Later, we learnt the Principal and Dunwell had had a massive show-down about the*

before my eyes, and I nearly rammed into the wavering drunk who was now staggering on the right side of the wide road. The drunk lurched towards my cycle and I barely swerved away in time, fighting to retain my hold on the rat-eaten, black plastic hand-grips. There was a slapping sound on the road behind me.

I immediately knew that Fatty Grewal had jumped off my cycle's carrier, as I felt the cycle suddenly become lighter and more manoeuverable. I had passed the drunk so I depressed both hand brakes and stopped the bicycle. I could hear Fatty's voice as he began to loudly chide the first drunk. Seeing that an exciting situation was brewing, the other drunk staggered up close to his inebriated companion. Gaining confidence from the presence of one another, they began to argue with Fatty in heavily slurring voices. At that moment, Kajla and I stepped in and broke up the ongoing, verbal brawl. Although the second drunk kept threatening us with physical violence, he seemed to be having a terrible time staying on his feet and swayed from side to side, like a ship in a storm.

Quickly looking back, we were relieved that Mr. HD Puri had not caught up with us. However, we knew we had to move fast to be in Capri Cinema Hall by 9 p.m. to see the film trailers of yet-to-be-released films that were screened before the movie being screened. Knowing, that '*discretion was the better part of valour*', Kajla

---

disturbance caused to classes due to the loud trumpet music. The Principal finally forced Dunwell to stuff a 'choke' and muzzle the trumpet horn. However, we knew Dunwell had carried the day, as he continued to play the trumpet in class and entertain us – of course with its 'choke' that greatly reduced the pleasant sounds.

and I physically pulled Fatty back to my bicycle. Encouraged by our hasty withdrawal, we could barely control our laughter as we saw one of the drunks blow bubbles as he drunkenly tried to hurl choicest abuses at us. The other drunk reached down to find a stone to hurl at us, but he could not find a stone on the clean road surface. However, due to the exertions he lost his balance, flapped down, and lay still as he sprawled on the road. The bubble blower ceased his attempted abuses and gallantly moved to help his flattened friend. Shaking a fist at the downed bubble-man, Fatty hopped onto the carrier of my bicycle. I pedalled very hard and tried to put a maximum distance between the two drunks and ourselves.

Luckily, there was a down-slope, and the wide road curved towards Bindal Bridge. Due to the down slope and our furious pedalling, we had attained an incredibly fast speed and the breeze fanned our faces pleasurably.

'*Slow down*! *SLOW DOWN KHALSEY*!' yelled a very nervous Fatty from behind me, as we hurtled towards the bridge at a crazy pace.

With the speed at which we were travelling, I was sure to hit the bridge-railings and cart-wheel into the deep and dry river bed. Quickly realising the folly due to our high speed, I tightly grabbed hold of the handle-bars with all my might and leaned over to the left, like a circus cyclist. The madly hurtling cycle swerved to the left and we barely avoided the bridge railings and swung safely onto the bridge.

I looked back at Fatty and said with great pride,

'*Fatty, did you enjoy the ride? Kya cycling ki hamne!*"

Having just experienced a very traumatic ride, Fatty was least amused by my cheerful comment and mumbled softly, *'I'll show you life on the way back! You will then have to sit on the damned carrier.'*

I guffawed silently, for I knew on the way back it would be a mighty uphill climb and Fatty would be busy huffing and puffing, rather than think of tricks to unnerve me! Knowing we had left both Mr. HD Puri and the drunks well behind us, we brought our cycles alongside to each other and the three of us burst into loud laughter without a care in the world.

After a couple of minutes, we were near Capri Cinema Hall. As we dismounted from the cycles, we could see the front of the hall was well lit. We kept in the shadows and saw that a number of people were milling around the steps at the entrance. We could not see any RIMC Masters at the entrance, so we knew the coast was clear. Fatty Grewal was given some money by Kajla and he cautiously entered the lobby to purchase the movie tickets, while we wheeled the cycles to the Cycle Park at the side of the hall. There was already a long line of cycles parked on their stands along the low wall that ran along the boundary and parallel to the tall building of the cinema hall. After parking our cycles and paying the Cycle Park owner a princely sum of Re 1 per cycle, we walked to the furthermost door and waited in the darkness. Soon, Fatty arrived with three small tickets of the lowest monetary value and handed us one ticket each. The tickets were made of small, green coloured limp paper with a corrugated edge.

As we had the cheapest tickets, we entered the hall from the door that was nearest the gently curved, 70 mm screen. The screen was made of thick, dirty-white coloured plastic sheet with thousands of tiny perforations. The naked bulb above the door must have fused some time back and the entire area was in a general state of semi-darkness. It seemed odd as we were the only people entering from the darkened door. We called the gate keeper who was standing some distance away in a lighted area and smoking a *bidi.* He came up to us and we saw he was a middle-aged, scruffy man wearing a khaki cotton coat and frayed trousers that had once been a blue colour. He had a filthy, unkempt appearance, and mops of uncombed hair hung over his unshaven face. What immediately caught my attention was the gate keeper's constant scratching on his trouser covered leg with great vengeance. Something was really troubling him, as his right hand worked its way between the knee and groin. He took our tickets with the left hand and sharply swung his head towards the hall to indicate that we could enter.

While we were walking inside the hall, I stopped and quite innocently asked the gate keeper, '*Kya seat number hai, hamara*?'

At that, the surprised gate keeper's face cracked into a crafty grin and he announced to no one in particular, in a loud rasping voice. '*Kya seat number hai,*' looked us over and tried to imitate me, '*Sabse agli wali line ki ticket kharidte ho aur sharam nahin aati puchhte hue ki seat number kya hai* ?'

I felt a tight tug on my arm and realised Fatty was unceremoniously pulling me within the darkened hall. My conversation with the gate keeper had ended as suddenly as it had begun.

The hall was nearly empty as we walked down a gentle slope to the row of chairs that were closest to the screen. The unclean hall was murky and it smelt heavily of stale bidi smoke, probably a left-over from the previous 6 p.m. to 9 p.m. show. As we walked to our seats, peanut shells crunched loudly under our shoes. We put down three, upturned seats, nearest to the door and sat down to enjoy the movie. To sit near the door was an instinctively motivated reaction, as it would allow us to exit the hall rapidly, should the need arise. Once we had settled down on the hard seats covered with cheap, red coloured, rexine material, we had to make an effort to throw our heads back to be able to view the large screen that loomed just before us. Looking around us, I noticed two men were seated directly behind me and they were happily cracking and munching peanuts from a cone made of newspaper. The peanut shells were thrown down on the floor, to add to the filth. They were both totally bedraggled and wore dirty, crumpled, striped pyjamas. Their uncombed hair was literally standing on end. They both seemed to have come to the hall straight from bed! The one behind me lifted his bare feet to the back of my chair and an awful looking big toe was soon resting against my neck! Without looking back, I brushed his feet away with the back of my hand.

Happily, he did not react to my angry gesture and there was silence. I did not want to start another altercation after our recent run-in with the drunks!

Trailers of films that were to be screened in the hall were shown to us. Then, at around 9.30 p.m. the film *April Fool* began. The moment actress Saira Banu came on the screen, our striped pajama-clad neighbours let out a barrage of piercingly loud wolf whistles. Though the whistles had disturbed the peace and also annoyed us, we did not turn back to confront the groundnut-munching revellers. The movie played on for more than an hour and we sat there thoroughly enjoying our outing. I distinctly recollect the song that went '*April Fool banaya aur unko gussa aaya...*', when all of a sudden a whitish, transparent slide appeared on the screen, partially hiding the gyrating actress. Large black words splashed across the screen, 'ALL RIMC CADETS WILL GET UP'[6], leaving us horrified!

We were stunned and did not move, till Fatty got up and yelled, '*Run for it chaps, they know we're here.*'

On hearing him, we urgently rose to our feet and ran to the nearest closed door. When we stood up, our seats swung back with a loud bang that must have alerted anyone who was looking for us. Thankfully, the gate keeper was not at the door, so we kicked it open and ran outside.

From the edge of the balcony above us, Mr. HD

---

6 *We came to know later that Mr HD Puri had already flashed his innovative slide (asking RIMC cadets to get up) in two other Cinema Halls, without any luck. He had finally hit gold in Capri Cinema Hall.*

Puri's voice boomed, '*There they are running out. There are three of them. Pakro unko!*'

We knew Mr. HD Puri was being true to his reputation of never giving up a chase when he had smelt RIMC cadets were cutting bounds! He had apparently followed us to the hall and was now determined to catch us.

Outside the door it was dark and we were in a quandary about what to do. There wasn't enough time to get hold of our cycles and flee. If we decided to run for it, Mr. Puri would easily catch us as he would be mounted on his fast-moving Bullet motorbike. Suddenly, I spied a piece of cement gutter-pipe (about 5 ft wide and 5 ft long) that had been placed vertically and was being used as a large dust bin. We ran to the cement-concrete dust bin, hoisted ourselves over its edge, and jumped in. We landed on something soft and wet and crouched inside unmoving, in the darkness. Just then we heard the deep '*dhap*, *dhap*, *dhap*' of Mr. Puri's motor-bike, and a headlight lit up the area around the dustbin. The three of us just sat tight inside the dust bin and did not move. A horrible stink spread around us and assailed our nostrils. Cupping a hand over our nose did not help as the awful stench managed to filter through our tightly closed fingers. '*Dhap, dhap, dhap*' the motorcycle appeared to have turned and was moving away from us and proceeding towards the clock tower.

Desperately wanting to get a breath of fresh air, we climbed over the dustbin's edge and landed softly on the ground. It took us an effort to scrape our shoes on the ground to get the foul-smelling, gooey muck off.

'*Stop rubbing so hard or you'll leave your shoe soles behind*' joked Fatty Grewal.

'*Then we'll have to make a trip to Phuntru! Anyway, let us get the hell out of here and get the cycles,*' I said and began to walk towards the cycle park.

As I stepped forward, my shoes made loud squelching sounds and the horrid stench seemed to follow me to the cycle park. There were similar sounds coming from the shoes of the others, as well.

The cycle park owner asked us why we wanted to take our cycles before the movie had ended. But when he had smelt the horrible stench that emanated from us, he had frowned and covered his nose. Without looking at us, he turned his face away and waved an arm in the direction of the cycles. The awful stink we had picked up from the dustbin seemed to have overpowered him. We took our cycles and pedalled towards Bindal Bridge. Despite all the commotion, I had the presence of mind to tell Fatty Grewal it was his turn to ride the cycle, while I hopped onto the cycle's carrier. The return journey was uneventful till we reached near the huge bamboo trees adjacent to the Doon School swimming pool.

We heard the horrible '*dhup, dhup, dhup*' sound coming from behind us. As immediate action was needed to evade Mr. Puri, we swung the bikes towards the Bindal River and jumped off our cycles. There was a deep drop of about 20 feet or so into the Bindal River. We hurriedly wheeled the cycles to the edge, as sounds of the motor-bike engine increased menacingly. We knew Puri was closing in on us and the motor-bike headlight had begun to light up tops of the bamboo grove. We knew the situation had now become desperate. We also knew that we could not be caught by the master, or our days in school would become sheer hell! Thus, the desperate situation called for desperate measures! Without another word, we heaved the cycles over the edge and jumped after them, without a second thought.

As I went down, there was this horrible feeling in the pit of the stomach. It was like being suspended in mid-air, or like jumping off the top diving board in the school swimming pool. We heard the cycles clatter to a halt on a ledge somewhere lower down the cliff. Then I felt a sharp upward pull at the back of my shirt, my neck jerked upwards and I stopped falling. My back scraped against the sheer cliff face and my flailing feet found a small ledge. A cascade of small stones rubbed off the cliff-face and fell noisily into the darkness of the Bindal River, down below. From my suspended position, I could see numerous cement houses with bright electric lights, across the riverbed. I heard some fumbling below me and knew that Fatty and Kajla had stabilized themselves on some sort of a shallow ledge, below my dangling position. I softly called out to them and asked if they were alright.

'We're okay here but where the hell are you Khalsey?' asked Fatty.

He must have looked up in the direction of my voice, as suddenly there was a loud burst of laughter.

'Bloody hell!' they had exclaimed together, *'You're*

hanging from a branch, like a leg of mutton!'

Both Fatty and Kajla began to laugh madly. Their laughter was either out of relief that we were all safe or purely because I was hanging by my collar.

That was the time I knew my fall had been abruptly broken by my shirt being snagged on a strong branch, protruding from the sheer cliff. Thus, I was now suspended over the dry riverbed, with my heels digging into a small ledge. There was no more time to speculate on our ridiculous situation, for we heard a motor-bike's '*dhap, dhap, dhap*' sound from the edge directly above us.

Praying that both the branch and my terylene shirt would hold me, I hissed at the others, '*For God's sake, shut up. He's here!!*'

Mr. Puri must have surely peered intently, over the edge of the drop. When he didn't see us, Puri must have thought his eyes had played tricks, when he felt he had seen the three RIMC cadets on two cycles! We stayed the way we were, till we heard the motorbike depart towards RIMC. Slowly, we helped each other to the top and lay panting on the grass. Then Fatty and I went down cautiously and hefted up the two cycles. In the great excitement of our narrow cscapc, wc had almost forgotten about the hideous stench that was clinging to us. However, while bringing up the cycles it assailed us once more. Trying desperately to outrun the smell, we cycled like mad to get back as fast as possible.

Only once we were back on the road did we realise the damage our cycles had suffered from the terrible man-handling and from being tossed over the edge of the cliff. Damage to Fatty's cycle was minor. It had lost one plastic handle-grip and the carrier would now move around crazily under my weight. However, Kajla's cycle made a wretched sound of '*chung, chung, chung*' when wheeled forward. Its badly bent rim was grazing against the body of the cycle. We told Kajla to dismount from the cycle and laid it flat on the road. I picked up a large, rounded rock from the roadside and swung it against the offending cycle rim, '*bang! bang! bang!*' When we tried out the cycle after that, we found it moved both smoothly and silently. I was reminded of actor John Waye saying in the movie *Longest Day*, '*Anything that doesn't move, give it a bang!*' So, we did just that and were soon cycling merrily back to the cycle shop in Garhi market.

At the cycle shop, the lungi clad owner was wide awake and received us with a broad smile. The smile quickly disappeared when his expert eye saw the banging his dear cycle had taken. He started to question us, but suddenly took two steps back as our awful stench assailed him. He quickly forgot about the extra money he had planned to extract from us on seeing the brutalized cycles. Mr. *Lungi* covered his nose and urgently motioned to us to park the cycles and leave the shop.

On the way back to RIMC we recollected the adventurous outing and laughed loudly. We removed our filthy shoes and socks, and rinsed them repeatedly in the flowing waters of Garhi Nala. When we were relatively cleaner, we marched confidently to Ranjit Section Senior

Dormitory. We had so much to tell the other cadets about our adventures. There were so many *gups* we could now *maro* and impress everybody. It had all ended well and during our Arts class we would look at one another, say *'dhup, dhup, dhup'* and roll on our chairs with merry laughter. Mr. HD Puri will never know, that night how close he had come to achieving his life's ambition – catching RIMC cadets while they were cutting bounds!

The Chicken Raid

Like on every Sunday morning in RIMC, smartly dressed in our blue blazer, grey flannel trousers, and college tie we would troop back from the house of Ranjit Section Master, Mr. GS Bisht, after collecting our valuable treasure of pocket money, in the form of a dog-eared, dirty yellow coupon having the value of Re 1. After signing Mr. Bisht's register and collecting our valued coupon, with downcast and serious faces we had to hear his lengthy recriminations about the chaos we had created during the previous week. It would always amaze us to learn that Mr. Bisht (or Bhishti, as we fondly called him), already knew about every clandestine, hush-hush, project we had been working on. Invariably he would begin by solemnly announcing, '*Don't you boys get into any more trouble ......*'.

We would innocently look down at our unkempt shoes, keep a very straight face and solemnly listen to what was said by Bishti. We would put on such pathetic expressions on our faces, that butter wouldn't have melted in our mouths! Once we were at a safe distance from the Section Master's house, we would guffaw loudly, jump for joy, slap each other on the shoulder, and ask stupid questions like, '*Do you think Bishti really knows, or was he pulling fast ones?*', '*How could he have ever got a wind of our plans?*'

Numerous answers would be furnished by us for our own questions, but the sum total of all answers would be something like, '*No, he doesn't know a thing. Bishti is trying to be extra smart and bull-shit us!*'

On one particular Sunday morning, however, things were a bit different. We carefully thrust our precious Re 1 coupons, deep into the pocket of our gray flannel trousers, and walked quickly towards Ranjit Section. On the way kicked large *bajri* stones to score imaginary football goals. All along, mouth-watering visions of Vimto bottles and buns with their green and red speckled tootifruity pieces, assailed our innocent minds.

Suddenly, GS Kochhar emerged from nowhere, confronted me, and asked in a serious tone, '*Jasbir, you had promised to pay me with your pocket money this week, for my geometry box you borrowed on Wednesday. Even though you have ruined my new divider, I will not charge you for it. Give me the pocket money, NOW!*'

I remembered the entire scene well*. We had wanted to play darts on the trunk of a large tree near our class (Class III) and we desperately needed a divider. Kochar (called Kochhi by us) possessed a new geometry box, but he was very possessive of it. He would literally guard the geometry box and its contents *with his life*! Thus, we never entertained any hopes of spiriting away his divider. Kochhi had bluntly refused to part with any contents of the geometry box. But, from his body language I had learnt he would agree to our borrowing the entire box, but for a hefty fee. Since I had been given the mission to procure either a divider or his entire geometry box for our planned darts game, I began to badger Kochhi. I used all my skills, but still, I could not make any headway with our friend. I had pleaded, cajoled, and even threatened him with dire consequences, but to no effect. When even my magnanimous offer of two dog-biscuits was spurned, I was forced to use my final weapon – an offer to Kochhi, which he could never refuse!

Cadet GS Kochhar (left) and I have a free-for-all fist-fight, after receiving our 'Sunday Morning Pocket Money'. Cadet DS (Fatty) Grewal tries desperately to push us apart.

In advance, I had offered him the Re 1 coupon I would be receiving from Mr. Bisht on the coming Sunday morning, for his complete geometry box. Kochhar had mulled over what I said and gladly agreed to the proposed deal. However, he had grudgingly handed us his geometry box. Taking the divider out of the geometry box, we had joyously commenced with our game of pseudo-darts. At a certain time in the game, Fatty hurled the open divider with all his might at the tree trunk. The divider hit the tree trunk at an angle, bounced, and landed at a fair distance away. When I went and picked up the divider, I noticed Fatty had caused us a major disaster. The divider had lost one of its sharp points and was horribly bent down the middle. Kochhi had been watching our darts game from a distance. On seeing Fatty's tragic shot, he had run up to us with a yell and inspected the horribly bent divider.

'*You'll have to pay for this! You have ruined my geometry box,*' he said, looking directly at me.

I was convinced I did not want to pay Kochhi Re 1 of my pocket money and then live like a ruddy hermit for rest of the coming week. So, I had a quiet discussion with Fatty Grewal, as we sauntered to the Mess. Fatty heard out my tale of woes and whispered a wonderful solution to the problem, in my ear.

Happily, I repeated a suitably modified form of the solution, to Kochhar, '*Look Kochhi, how would you like it if I paid you for the geometry box and for the damaged divider with some delicious chicken*?'

On listening to me, Kochhar had come to a sudden

stop and he seriously thought about what I had said. He was interested in my proposal, as there were still three days remaining before he would get our weekly share of chicken, in the mess!

'*Okay, but I want the chicken today itself,*' said Kochhar in an unreasonable manner, after giving a deep thought to what I had just said.

Fatty, Unni, Bhalla, and I quickly reviewed this grave problem that had loomed up. After a good thought, we decided to give Kochhar our acceptance. So, with a sweet smile I told Kochhar we were in agreement with his demand and he would receive the chicken, that very evening! As further confirmation to what I had said, Fatty, Unni, Bhalla, and others with us, seriously nodded their heads. Kochhar and I then seriously shook hands, to mark the finalization of our deal. I told Kochhar the plan in a nutshell. It had been decided that after dinner, we would raid Gwala's chicken coop, get ourselves a chicken and then roast the bird in the isolated, dry Nala bed, near Rifle Range.

Kochhar would get his roasted chicken, with only a small bite taken by each of us for all our efforts! Saying so, I had licked my lips in great anticipation of the chicken-treat. Kochhar was impressed with our plan but, he expressed his doubts about whether we would be able to bushwhack the bird from Gwala's Chicken Coop. I assured him that removing the chicken from the coop was going to be easy as we were experts at such activities. But, cooking the bird was going to be the difficult part of the plan! Since Fatty and Bhalla had claimed to have great culinary talents, I hoped that the cooking part too would be easily accomplished. We told Kochhar to be ready for the 'Chicken Raid', at 10 p.m., after we'd had our dinner. We had planned to wear games dress for the 'Chicken Raid'.

At 10 p.m., we briefly gathered in the locker room and then took off for the gymnasium. In one hand, Fatty was carrying a khaki jacket.

I asked Fatty why he was carrying the jacket, and he had just smiled and kept walking. *'You'll soon know,'* he said a little later.

At the gymnasium, we waited for about five minutes and quietly crossed the *bajri* covered pathway that led to the hedge-rows surrounding Mr. Jaswal's (Gwala's) house. We had barely settled down very quietly in the hedge, when lo and behold Gwala came out of his house onto the veranda. He was wearing a white *kurta* and pyjama. Standing on the veranda, he yawned noisily and then let out a series of explosive coughs.

From inside the house his annoyed wife had called, *'What are you doing outside? Do come inside immediately!'*

The hedge was dark and some light fell on it from the veranda. Gwala again stretched his limbs, opened the door, and went inside the house.

Without wasting any time, we quietly moved in the dark along the hedge towards Section Hospital. Then, we crossed the hedge through a gap and stepped on the dark veranda. Three rooms opened onto the veranda and comprised of an external kitchen and two store rooms. The veranda and rooms were in total darkness and it appeared that Gwala was seriously trying to avoid paying an exorbitant electricity bill! But, this was an insult to our sensibilities, as would-be 'poultry robbers'. We felt slighted by the fact that Gwala had not cared to switch on the lights to have proper security and protect his chicken run, from us!

A horrible smell was coming from the external kitchen, and we could easily guess Gwala was using it as our target – the 'Chicken Run'! We easily opened the Klik padlock, with the remaining pin of Kochhi's divider, and pushed open the doors of the 'Chicken Run'. As the doors opened, the smell immediately got worse and made us hurry on with our task. Fatty flashed a pencil torch-light around the room and we saw about 20 large chickens sitting motionless on wooden racks along the walls. Fatty could be seen smiling widely, as he turned back and flashed a thumbs-up sign at us. Suddenly, there was a noisy flapping of wings in the room, followed by the muted squawking of a chicken. Fatty turned the torch on himself and looked at me. He was smiling and held the jacket firmly under his arm.

He patted the jacket and mouthed silent words to me, '*You wanted to know why I was carrying the jacket. It is for this purpose, Khalsey!*'

Having got our chicken, we hurriedly trooped out of Gwala's poultry, crossed the hedge, and headed back to our dorm. On the way, we stopped near the boilers, where Fatty and I skinned and cleaned the chicken. We then went into a tub-baths room, turned on a faucet, and washed the skinned bird and ourselves of its feathers and blood in the tub. Kochhi was getting more and more excited knowing that things were actually working out and we had not been fooling him all along.

Now, began the important part of our mission – cooking the bird! Fatty had made adequate arrangements for this important part of the plan. He had borrowed an old and dented, aluminium cooking pot from the 'head waiter', Bachhan Singh, along with some condiments. The condiments and salt were wrapped in a piece of newspaper. As we hid in the hedgerows, Fatty handed me the wet chicken and surreptitiously entered the locker room of Ranjit Section Senior Dorm. Opening the cellar, he extracted the precious cooking pot, packet of condiments, and a bottle of water. Happily waving the spoils, he returned to us in the hedgerows. He had also found a thin, yellow, polythene bag to carry the chicken, which he threw across to me. I quickly put the wet chicken into the plastic bag and we moved off towards the Rifle Range. Just then, there was a shrill call of *'OOH! OOOOOH!'* and we knew our old friend, the wise, old owl, was flying from tree to tree in the dark and moving with us to Rifle Range! We smiled among ourselves, for we knew the owl brought luck during our nocturnal adventures. Kochhi had been very surprised by the owl's calls, but we had no time to stop and explain our close links with the ruddy owl! So we had smiled to ourselves and quickly walked past the Masters' houses and descended into the dark and deeply wooded nala before the Rifle Range.

On reaching the *nala*, we found a nice spot and made ourselves comfortable on the dry sandy bed. We placed three rocks on the sand, collected some dry twigs, and started a fire. Once the fire was blazing away merrily, Fatty and Anil Bhalla poured water from the bottle into the cooking pot and followed it with the chicken and condiments. The pot was placed on three rocks and left to boil, while we sat around the fire and indulged in aimless chatter. We cut jokes on our friends and staff members. Time passed rapidly, as we sat on the dark, *nala* bed. Soon, the chicken had boiled nicely and had become quite soft. Fatty removed the chicken from the pot and threw away the water in which the chicken had boiled.

Then, he and Bhalla easily tore up the boiled chicken into many parts and put the pieces back into the empty pot. Fatty and Bhalla liberally rubbed the remaining condiments on the chicken pieces and held them over the flames to roast. An enticing smell soon rose from the roasting chicken pieces. As the flames were getting weak, I rose up to collect more dry twigs to keep our fire ablaze. Soon, the chicken pieces were well roasted and we put them back in the empty cooking pot.

Fatty put all the salt in the cooking pot that contained the roasted chicken pieces and began to sharply shake the pot. The chicken pieces moved to and fro with a pleasant sound and were soon well salted.

Fatty said to Kochhi, '*All cooked and complete, Sir! Shall we now have a piece of chicken each, as we had agreed?*'

Much as he would have liked to avoid our feast,

Kochhi had no option but to nod his head meekly and affirm that we could each have a piece of chicken! So, we dug into the pot and extracted a large and juicy piece each. The chicken was tough and slightly raw, but it did not matter and we ate our piece with great relish. We told Fatty the chicken was indeed delicious! Kochhar then collected the remaining pieces of roasted chicken from the cooking pot and placed them on a couple of hankies he had tied together for the purpose. With our mission successfully completed, we stamped out the fire, lifted the cooking pot and our empty bottle, and made our way silently back to our dormitory.

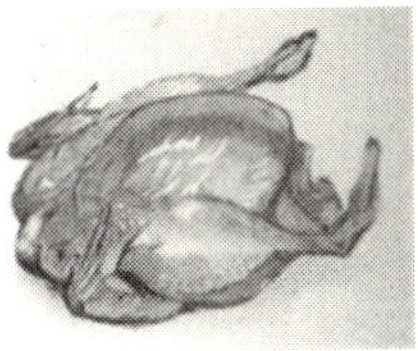

Our boiled chicken

We were glad we had finally paid back Kochhi with the cooked chicken and ended the terribly one-sided contract. Though we had sadly watched Kochhi pack the chicken pieces and carry them off, the uppermost concern in our minds was to safely return unseen to our dormitory and dive into our beds. On the way back there was complete silence all around us. Even the sound of the empty, cooking pot rubbing against twigs and branches, seemed to be incredibly loud, and we had to warn Fatty to be careful! Our friend, the wise, old owl seemed to have flown off to some safe tree, and we knew it would meet us again during our next adventure! On reaching our dormitory we snuggled deeper into our beds, quite proud of ourselves and happy at our successfully completed mission. We wanted to pat ourselves on the back for having raided Gwala's 'Chicken Run' and cooked the bird, without being caught in the act!

Now it was time to silently sound off the *'three cheers for ourselves – hip, hip hooray.'*

With that fine thought we drifted off into a sound sleep – tomorrow was another day and after the PT class, we would think up another adventure!

The Three Ostrich Feathers Trophy

At night, somewhere around 12 March 1963 or '64, we, the cadets of Ranjit Section, were thoroughly dejected as we trooped to the mess from the open air theatre next to the Principal's house, located at a corner of RIMC behind the convocation hall. The boxing finals had just gotten over and our hopes of winning the boxing trophy had been dashed to the ground – thoroughly smashed by Shivaji Section, as badly as the noses and chins of our boxers, with Arvind (Tinda) Kumar our classmate being declared the best boxer. That fellow, Tinda, may have been just four feet tall, but he could jump up and execute a nasty uppercut on an opponent twice his height and deliver a knockout blow.

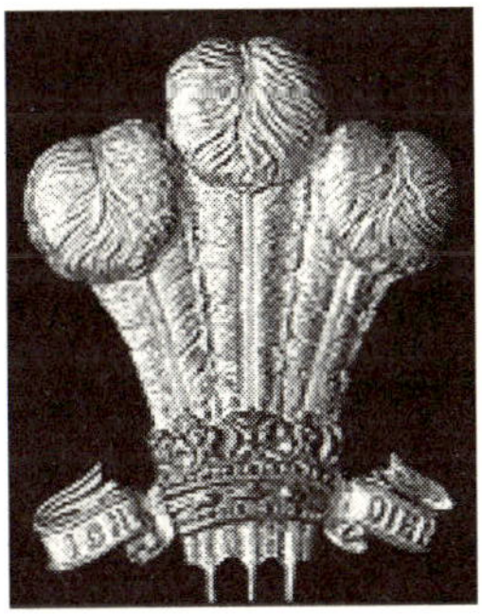

The large, silver Three Ostrich Feathers crest

We were proud of Tinda, our classmate, but the fellow was in the wrong section! He was in Shivaji Section and they had just won the ruddy boxing championship!

To further our humiliation, there was lot of cheering from Shivaji Section in the dining hall and finally, they arose from their chairs simultaneously and went around the mess tapping the rest of us seated cadets of other sections on our heads with tablespoons that they brandished with great pride and zest. As the crescendo of cheering reached an ear-splitting level, the wooden tables were tapped noisily with spoons in perfect rhythm. '*Jeet gaya bhai jeet gaya, Shivaji Section jeet gaya,*' they jeered.

As cadets of Ranjit Section, our humiliation was complete, as we quietly sat at our tables and repeatedly received good-hearted knocks on our heads with tablespoons. That is when, a few of us decided to launch a retaliatory strike, as we knew that our colleagues from Shivaji Section would regularly tease us and make our lives most miserable in class, till the next tournament. But, what were we to do to retrieve the situation? The loud cacophony of cheering made it even more difficult for us to think and come up with an answer.

We, thus, remembered the advice of our sagacious, swashbuckling, and very inspiring Administrative Officer (AO). Capt KC Anand, and decided to implement his golden words, '*Whenever you find yourself seized with a problem and there is no solution in sight, then sleep over the matter and you'll find the answer you're looking for during the next morning.*'[7]

Next morning was a Sunday and we met in the mess, invigorated by a sound sleep that possibly had been induced by the knocks we had received on our heads with spoons wielded by the joyful cadets of Shivaji Section. What immediately caught our eye was the beautiful silver trophy kept on the centre table next to the seat of Cadet Captain. The large silver trophy was a beautiful replica of three curved ostrich feathers gathered in a crown, it was the old RIMC crest with *Ich Dien* (I Serve) inscribed below as the motto. We could never forget the number of front-rolls we had executed on bricks embedded at an angle and bordering the quadrangle, for misspelling the Latin motto of *Ich Dien* as *Itch Dien!* The ostrich feathers had recently been replaced by three peacock feathers, thereby removing some of the colonial linkages of RIMC's past. The beautiful trophy on the centre table sparked off our fuse and set in motion our juvenile plans for retaliation and retribution. In hushed tones we discussed and finalized our plans with utter glee and we gloated on our great brain-wave. We had not heard of psy-war in those days, but our minds were kept churlishly fertile with scotch eggs. Even at that young age we were aware that the war we had to fight, could only be won by using the 'dirty tricks department'!

Like all good battle plans, the plan we hatched was very simple and we counted on it to work wonders in our favour. Our aim was to target the entire Shivaji Section, using the name of their venerable Section Master

---

[7] *In those days the only man in uniform in RIMC was the AO.*

as a scapegoat. We decided to launch a whispering campaign that would be started with the positive investment of a free Vimto[8] and buns to a well-known gossip monger from Pratap Section. We were sure he would readily spread the word and Shivaji Section would become the laughing stock of RIMC. The gossip monger would be told very seriously that the Three Ostrich Feathers trophy in the mess, encased in a glass box, was a fake. We hoped to spread the word that the venerable and exemplary Section Master of Shivaji Section had replaced the large and heavy silver Ostrich Feathers trophy with an old ostrich feathers beret cap badge. To ensure that the fraud was not discovered, we planned to spread the word (psy-war) that he had mischievously replaced the plain glass cover that surrounded the trophy with sheets of magnifying glass. We had planned to spread the word that the Section Master had been ably assisted in his evil enterprise by a mess-waiter nick-named Sondae[9]. It was to be seriously suggested that the actual silver trophy had been sold to a *kabadi* in the depths of Paltan Bazaar and that the proceeds were to benefit both the Section Master and cadets. We spread the word that cadets of Shivaji Section were receiving Rs 3 every Sunday, while cadets of all other sections were given only the measly Re 1 as pocket money!

---

8 *The Coke and Pepsi of our times, bottled by the venerable contractor who ran the cafeteria was called Vimto. Vimto was an incredible drink, the true elixir of our youth. One sip transported one to heaven.,*

9 *We had a big grudge against 'Sondae', the long nosed mess waiter who was thoroughly disliked only because he outright refused to serve us with 'extra' cutlets and scotch eggs. He would even run to 'sneak' about our pestering to Thopleh, the imposing Butler, whom we unjustly suspected of eating all the extra scotch eggs himself.*

Our psy-war using the mole from Pratap Section worked for a while. It demoralised Shivaji and they neither laid claim to the trophy nor shifted it to their side of the mess. They were silent and bore the brunt of all the jeering stoically. The poor Section Master, the smartest of the four Section Masters, unfortunately, got a bad name because of our mischief – he was an honourable man. But our battle plan only produced short-term results. When they went to claim their share of the loot, the Rs 3 pocket money which they felt was their rightful share, their Section Master only gave them the same Re 1, just like all other Section Masters.

Afterward, we invented a slogan, '*Gali gali mein shor hai, ki Shivaji Section chor hai.*'

We tried more psy-war to demoralise the enemy, but it did not last very long.

Today, half a century later, all I can say with surety is that our grand plan was not a total failure. Every time when senior *Rimcollians* go to RIMC and look at the Three Ostrich Feathers trophy, they wonder with nostalgia whether there is a magnifying glass covering the trophy and whether it is indeed a cap badge masquerading as a trophy! Thus, the mystery of the Three Ostrich Feathers trophy continues to this day. Old fogies still ask with a merry chuckle, '*Who stole the Three Ostrich Feathers trophy?*'

The only one who really knows the truth is Mamu, our classmate, who went on to become the Commandant and whose job it was to have the ruddy trophy polished. We have sworn Mamu to secrecy, and we humbly seek forgiveness from the venerable Section Master of Shivaji for taking his name in vain. He was genuinely a good man, and we rogues had unfairly ruined his reputation.

Squash by Night

During our time in RIMC, it had become an obsession to win all inter-section games and sports competitions; with the ultimate aim to win the overall championship. We wanted to be the Champion Section and proudly wear our lanyard on the right shoulder of OG walking-out uniforms! A detailed tally of points gained and lost was maintained in our overall position in various games and sports. We periodically debated our chances to win a particular championship and decided on a particular manner to play a respective game, for achieving success. So, we definitely had to win the approaching inter-section squash championship, to stay in the race to become Champion Section!

One Sunday, the Section Commander called all senior cadets of the sections together and told us it was imperative to win the squash championship to stay in the running, for winning the overall championship.

After taking our views, he ended by asserting, '*We have to win the squash trophy, to remain in running for the overall championship.*'

The section squash team had been selected earlier,

but more practice was needed. Thus, on dispersing we immediately went to our cupboards to check our squash rackets and squash balls, we needed for the practice sessions. Since the college had only one squash court, we faced a major problem regarding the allotment of time for our practice sessions. Teams of all three sections were to be granted adequate time for practice sessions, which were to be held during games period. Thus, all sections were allotted inadequate time for practice. So, we went to the adjoining racket-court to conduct our practice, but we found it was too large and dark, and it had inadequate lighting. Also, the walls had an uneven surface that caused the squash ball to rebound at crazy angles! So, we came up with the idea, to conduct our practice sessions in the squash court itself, during early hours of the morning. After squash practice, we planned to proceed directly for our morning PT class.

That evening, luckily, dinner was continental style consisting of a soup, two vegetable cutlets, baked vegetables, and bread slices. We exchanged conspiratorial glances, and each of us quickly, wrapping a cutlet and two slices of bread in our handkerchiefs. We were careful, not to be seen by either the other cadets or hawk-eyed Thopleh, the portly butler. The vegetable cutlet was expertly crushed between two slices of bread to make a delicious sandwich. To make it look very normal, we made a big show of relishing the other cutlet, baked vegetables, bread slices, and the dessert.

After the light meal, we went to our dormitory, excitedly set the alarm for 2.30 a.m., and climbed into bed to get some sleep. We were promptly awake when the alarm sounded and quickly changed into PT kit. We pulled out our squash raquets and squash balls from the cooler. The cooler was a large wall cupboard in the locker room. It was deep and had adequate space. The term cooler had been taken from a World War II movie, *The Great Escape*, which we had watched. In the movie, prisoners who did something wrong were locked in the cooler as punishment.

It was a dark, moonless, and cool night. Carrying our squash gear and the precious sandwiches, five cadets in PT kit silently slipped into the night, from Ranjit Section Middle Dormitory. We proceeded past the water boilers of Ranjit Section and cadets sleeping soundly in Shivaji Section dormitories. We crossed the large ground between Holding Section and Section Hospital and proceeded to the Squash Court. As we were crossing the large playground, a grey coloured owl gave a loud, hoot that shattered the silence of the night. The owl had been startled on seeing five ghostly apparitions in white, walking in a single file, each one carrying a wooden raquet and small packet of sandwiches.

On reaching the squash court, one of us turned on the powerful lights and two cadets entered the court. The rest of us climbed the short flight of wooden stairs and sat on benches in the small balcony. The cadets down below in the squash court looked up and asked us for a ball. We threw down the small, black rubber ball with a yellow dot, and the practice session commenced. Soon, the sharp sounds of the squash ball hitting the wall were reverberating loudly, in the silent night. Initially, we were worried that the bright lights of the squash court would be seen and sounds of the game being played would be heard by someone but, gradually we gained confidence and forgot about our fears.

We continued with our practice session and merrily munched into our sandwiches, during the breaks in our play. The sandwiches tasted nice and we silently thanked Thopleh and the mess staff. We never realised how fast time flew, for soon it was daylight and time for us to proceed to the parade ground for our morning PT fall-in. Moving on the run, we would put our squash gear in the cooler and proceed to the parade ground. We were perspiring heavily after the intense squash practice, and were well warmed up for the PT class! However, the other cadets were fresh and well-groomed. They looked at the five of us rather derisively, and appeared somewhat satisfied when we told them we had been for an early morning run!

This incident highlights the great spirit of adventure that exists in cadets of RIMC, and their ability and great desire to brave all kinds of adversities in order to achieve their goals. The time of day or night doesn't matter, as long as the task is accomplished. This great quality of fearlessness is ideally suited for combat operations and victory in battle.

Ghosts of the Quadrangle

March 1966 was a fine time to be in RIMC, Dehradun. We were in our final term and ready to join NDA, Kharakvasla, after successfully qualifying in the scary UPSC written examination and the Services Selection Board test. The *Rimcollians* Meet on 13 and 14 March had gone off well and we were fortunate the Chief Guest, Nawab Zafar Alam of Rampur, had declared 15 March as a school holiday.

Cadet Arun Mamgain and I had stood together and listened in amazement as the portly Nawab Sahib had raised his right fist in the air, looked at the blue sky, and shouted in a deep, baritone voice, '*Three cheers for RIMC, Heep, Heep Hurray!*'

Though we were excited when Mr. Zafar Alam declared 15 March as a school holiday, my personal joy knew no bounds as 15 March is my birthday. Each year in school, I used to wait expectantly for the chief guest to declare 15 March as a holiday, so that the good time could continue after the Old Boy's meet was over. Some of the chief guests were very condescending when approached by the motivated Cadet Captain, while others would nod their heads, have a quick word with Mr. SP Sharma, the Principal, and make a short speech that extolled on the need to attend classes on 15 March, study hard, and do well in life! In short, there was to be no holiday! After nearly half a century of wondering, I am yet to understand how, by attending routine classes on 15 March, we could become toppers in our class!

With a holiday having been declared on 15 March 1966, we had a leisurely breakfast and then ambled to No.1 Cricket Ground, where a cricket match against 58 Gorkha Training Centre [GTC] was in progress. The school team had won the toss and was batting.

A motley crowd of spectators sat on the grassy slopes near Pratap Section, and occasionally a cheer went up in unison, '*Jeetega bhai jeetega, RIMC jeetega!*'

We (Cadets DS *Fatty* Grewal, AS Kajla, HS *Bugle* Vaid, and me) sat on the small slope beside the road and near the letterbox. There were a few junior cadets from Pratap Section and Ranjit Section sitting near us. Kajla and Vaid began to talk loudly of the 'headless horseman' who was known to gallop madly across the quadrangle to sound the historic, brass, school bell with his drawn sword[10]. The spectacle of the ghostly gallop supposedly took take place at the stroke of midnight, whenever it

---

[10]*It was widely rumoured that on one night, the 'headless horseman' had swiped Nannu the bell-bearer on his head with the flat portion of his sword, causing Nannu to become a diehard addict of the firebrand Tharra from Garhi Baz hool Bell pre maturely, thereby sounding an early end to the day's classes, much to the annoyance of our teachers! However, it was whispered that some cadets would deliberately tell Nannu the wrong time to make him sound the bell prematurely, and terminate the day's classes or evening prep!*

was a Friday/Saturday night. The young cadets sitting beside us seemed to be very interested in the ghost stories we were relating, for they edged closer to us and began to ask serious questions about the ghostly apparition.

That is when I casually announced that the 'headless horseman' had not been seen for the last couple of years. It seemed he had been replaced by a pair of tall ghosts who walked from the Cadet Captain's Room, across the quadrangle, and sounded the school bell once, exactly at midnight on every Friday/Saturday night. These two ghosts were known to dress in flowing white robes and carry a lit candle in each hand. By now, the gathering around us had increased manifold and the cricket match seemed to be holding only secondary interest, as compared with our interesting ghost tales. Very seriously Vaid added that since it was Friday, it was very likely the ghosts would appear that night. This caused a deep murmur of heightened interest and our impromptu audience began to excitedly chatter amongst themselves.

Finding a suitable opportunity, we rose and quietly moved back to our dormitory (Ranjit Section Senior Dormitory). We laughed amongst ourselves and clapped with glee when we thought of the fools we had made of the junior cadets. Once we had reached our dormitory, we seriously thought about the ghost act we were to perform that night. Sitting on the stairs outside the dormitory, it was decided that *Bugle* Vaid and I would impersonate the two ghosts at midnight. We were to drape ourselves in white bedsheets, open our long hair before our faces and carry lit candles in both hands. We took

CS Lehl, Cadet Captain, into confidence and reached his room about 15 minutes before midnight.

Dressed in PT kit, Vaid and I and quietly slipped inside the Cadet Captain's room. We were carrying a bedsheet each and were closely followed by Fatty Grewal who held four candles and a matchbox in his hands. Checking his wristwatch, Fatty told us to drape the bedsheets and commence our ghost-act. We draped the white bedsheets over our shoulders and loosened our top knots so that our long hair completely covered our faces. We could barely see through our hair, but it did not really matter as it helped in the ghost-act. Fatty handed each of us two lit candles and gave us a gentle push to commence our performance. Before we knew it, Vaid and I were walking down the steps in front of Cadet Capt's Room and entering the quadrangle. In addition to the lit candles, I was also carrying a short, stout staff with which I was to pound the large brass bell at the other end of the quadrangle.

Cadet Capt CS Lehl

Once the grass of the Quadrangle had touched our PT shoes, we walked abreast with our shoulders nearly touching one another. From the corners of our eyes, we could see anxious faces of cadets peering out from Ranjit Section Junior Dormitory, Mixed Dormitory, and Pratap Section. '*Let's make some sound to scare the jokers,*' I hissed at Vaid and let out a horrible screech.

The eerie sound I had emitted, totally surprised me and soon Vaid too joined in with an even more hopeless wail. We swayed our candles from side to side and cast weird shadows on the grass. We were having fun and it all seemed to be going well, despite our outrageous shrieks. Wearing their striped pyjama suits, cadets could be seen hiding behind whatever cover they could find. They watched us in awe from all the dormitories adjoining the quadrangle. It was all going so well when suddenly the unthinkable happened and tragedy struck our ghost-act. *Bugle* Vaid stepped on his bedsheet, muttered a loud curse, and came crashing down to the ground. His candles fell on the grass and were snuffed out immediately.

I was so stunned that I halted - both my movements and by the absurd wail I was emitting. A loud mumble was heard from the awestruck cadets watching us from their hiding places. The mumble quickly changed to loud shouts.

I distinctly heard, '*Bloody hell! They are NOT ghosts!*' and '*Maro inko, chhodna mat!*'

I heard the sounds of slippers landing on cement and *bajri* and soon a horde of shouting cadets were charging into the quadrangle, from three directions. Vaid was still on the ground, struggling with both his open hair and the offending bedsheet. I realised that discretion was the better part of valour, and quickly decided to save my skin. While Vaid was trying to disentangle himself from the bedsheet, he made horrible sounds, as if he was being strangled. I threw down my candles, bed-sheet, and stout staff quickly twisted my hair into a top-knot and ran at full pelt across the quadrangle and towards the Junior Ante-Room. Luckily for me, the onrushing swarm of cadets found the downed figure of *Bugle* Vaid a more attractive option and did not pursue me. As I ran, I could hear Vaid's loud yells and knew he had been caught and was being soundly thrashed. Without a backward glance, I literally flew like a bat out of hell, past the college's office, the flag pole, and the open-air theatre. I finally regained my confidence and slowed to a walk, near the *gobar gas* plant. With hands on my hips, I puffed hard and listened intently. There was silence all around me – I was happy that I could not hear any sounds of my pursuers. Cautiously, I tramped back to Ranjit Section and crept into the locker room of Senior Dormitory. Here I found the tall figure of a soundly-thrashed Vaid, surrounded by many Ranjit Section cadets. Everyone was laughing and slapping Vaid on the back. They were very pleased to see me and sat me down on the wooden lockers. Gradually I learnt what had happened in the quadrangle, after Vaid's tragic fall. Following the initial kicks and blows, I was told Vaid had been saved from further harm by the timely arrival of the Cadet Captain. Horrified on seeing Vaid's bloated face I had asked him the reason why he had not mentioned his seniority and blasted the juniors, who seemed to have gone berserk in the quadrangle.

Vaid's reply had us all guffawing madly.

He said softly, '*I did try! I shouted at the juniors and told them they would be taken to task for assaulting a senior cadet.*'

The juniors had promptly replied with big smiles on their faces, '*What 'senior cadet' are you talking about, Sir? We were only thrashing a ruddy ghost!*'

Tall Stands the Soldier

The Kumaon Regiment of the Indian Army and Rashtriya Indian Military College (RIMC - Dehradun) share a common history that goes back many decades and wars. Personalities like Ambassador and Col Niranjan Singh Gill, Gen KS Thimayya, DSO, Lt Gen K Bahadur Singh, MBE, Maj Somnath Sharma, PVC, and many others have proudly donned both the Three Ostrich/Peacock Feathers and Russel's Lion badges on their uniforms. However, this article is about a unique *Rimcollian* and his remarkable story of sheer perseverance and courage. I have been witness to it all, as we were together in Ranjit Section, RIMC, and later I too have served for long years in the Kumaon Regiment.

My recollections begin during the rainy day in August 1962 at RIMC, Dehradun. A slim, young, lad extended his hand and told me we were from the same section – Ranjit Section – and asked if we would be friends. As a fresher, I could never have realised the handshake would herald a lasting friendship that has lasted for more than 40 years. The long years of knowing my friend has allowed me to be a witness to his deep courage and perseverance. I write about a wonderful human being named Maj Gen (retired) Naginder Singh. When I recently told him over the phone, I was going to write about him, I could literally imagine him shaking his head. With great humility he told me to write about something else, as he did not deserve to appear in such an article! It was so typical of him to try and hide in the shadows after a spectacular deed. Well, this story is not about a flash-in-the-pan kind of performance, rather it highlights the perseverance and courage he has displayed all through his years in uniform (1962 to 2010) – it is akin to a well-run cross-country race or a cadet's supreme efforts during a polo-post race[11]!

Being in the same Section at RIMC allowed me to be with Naginder during numerous friendly misdemeanors like 'Cutting Bounds', 'Ganna Raids', 'Lifting birds from chicken coops in Master's houses and cooking them in the thickly wooded premises of the Rifle Range'. I remember concealing bread slices and oval shaped vegetable cutlets during our dinner and taking them out of the mess to our dormitory. We would, then, crush the cutlets between the slices to rig up improvised sandwiches for our early morning snacks. We would be up at 2.30 a.m. and quietly sneak out to the squash court, with our squash raquets, precious squash ball and the sandwiches. After switching on the powerful lights we would play on till we were exhausted. Then, we would eat our crushed-cutlet sandwiches and return to our dormitory,

---

11 *'Polo-Post' was the abbreviated form of 'Polo-Ground & Post – Office'. The name of the grueling cross country route for senior cadets in RIMC.*

in time for morning tea and PT class.

During the term break, we would travel together by train to Pathankot, which was the railhead at the time. Often, Anil Bhalla[12] would also accompany us up to Jammu. At Pathankot, we would board the officer's bus and proceed into J&K. Naginder would travel to Jammu, where his father was posted, while I went on to Srinagar. As we travelled along, we would dissect all happenings in school and make great plans for the next term. Studies were never discussed and we concentrated on adventure, games, and some 'mischievous stuff' like cutting bounds and various raids.

We were fortunate to qualify in the written exam for admission to NDA and the Services Selection Board tests. Finally, school days were over and we reached NDA, Kharakvasla. I am not aware of details, but I knew Naginder had been withdrawn from NDA, for some petty misdemeanour.

Thereafter, life went on and I got busy with combat operations in East Pakistan and Nagaland. Naginder was off my screen till I was posted to Indian Military Academy (IMA), Dehradun, as an instructor in 1976. One of my first duties in IMA was to oversee the issue of clothing to new Gentleman Cadets (GCs). I was pleasantly surprised to find a familiar face with a 'mess-tin hair cut', wearing grossly ill-fitting shorts and standing in line with the new GCs. Of all the people I could have

---

[12] *Anil Bhalla was commissioned in 4 Gorkha Rifles. During India-Pakistan War, 1971, he was wounded and had to lose a leg. He is settled in Calcutta where he runs a Transport business.*

imagined, it was Naginder! After our happy meeting we sat down together for a while and exchanged notes.

I had learnt from others, that after leaving NDA, Naginder had joined 13 Kumaon as a *jawan* and had fought in the India-Pakistan War, 1971. At that time, the Adjutant of 13 Kumaon was a *Rimcollian* named Capt (later Col) PV Singh. During the war, Naginder was wounded in action, in the western desert. After the 1971 war was over, Naginder joined Army Cadet College (ACC), Pune, and resolutely underwent the tough training. After qualifying from ACC, he joined IMA, Dehradun, where I had met him. I had been posted out of IMA when I learnt with joy that Naginder had been commissioned in a Regiment of Armoured Corps.

He went through his service career as an outstanding officer and was seconded to Defence Research & Development Organisation (DRDO). He retired recently in the rank of Maj Gen. Anyone else may have given up on the way or lost his fighting spirit but, not Naginder! From a cadet in RIMC, Dehradun, to the lofty stature of a two-star general officer in our army, entails a truly long and difficult journey. However, he constantly persevered and courageously continued till he had attained the heights that all personnel who don service uniforms and aspire to achieve their dreams during their careers. With his extraordinary grit, Naginder has proved to one and all that a dedicated soldier can rise to any lofty heights if they have courage and perseverance.

May young men from RIMC, Kumaon Regiment, and other walks of life look up to this soft-spoken hero and try to emulate his courageous ways for the betterment of lives and careers.

Let Us Leave a Mark!

On a lazy Sunday morning in early 1966, we were sitting on the steps outside Ranjit Section Senior Dormitory, lazing around and doing nothing in particular! We had just had a hearty Sunday breakfast and the sun was nice and warm. Life seemed really good and it couldn't have been better. Then we saw some studious friends, wearing games kit, pass us by with books in their hands. They were seriously walking towards our class (V-A) in Education Block, to prepare for the forthcoming Indian School Certificate (ISC) Examination. Absurdly, we yelled at them and poked fun at their outlandish intentions to go to class on a Sunday and study!

'*They must be quite mad to go to class on Sunday*,' said Fatty Grewal [1], smiling broadly and shaking his head from side to side.

One of the studious cadets must have heard Fatty's comment, for he stopped and said, '*Fatty Grewal, you will never learn! Yes, we're going to class to study. Unlike you, we will do very well in the ISC exam and leave a mark for others to follow. We will make everyone proud of us, just you wait and see.*'

The studious cadet's remarks induced an instant peal of laughter from us, followed by loud jeers.

After the group of cadets had gone past us and proceeded towards Education Block, I enquired, '*What did he mean by saying they're going to leave a mark? Why don't we do something outstanding as well – something that will be remembered for many, many years to come?*'

Again there was a round of bawdy laughter followed by more jeers.

Fatty looked at me intently and said, '*Khalsey, I hope you are okay? Forget about leaving a mark. All you have to do is look at this fellow's bloody legs,*' he said pointing at Unni's legs, laughing profusely. '*You will see the terrible marks!*'

Turning to me again he said, '*In any case, you can be sure that no one is going to remember your stupid hand-springs!*' There was another round of raucous laughter, while I pretended to be peeved.

Our group from Ranjit Section was known to shy away from academic pursuits, and as a result, we generally performed rather badly in the periodic phase tests. On the other hand, we would normally perform well in games and other extra-curricular activities. However, we could even perform adequately in academics, if we had a challenge or had seriously decided to do well in our studies. Academics was not on our minds very often, though we rarely failed in any subject. Sometimes things did not go well for us; our mischief was discovered and we even got caned. But, we had learnt to laugh off our travails and to remain happy! A few weeks earlier, we had engaged ourselves in a crazy adventure to fabricate and launch a homemade, liquid fuel rocket! Some friends, the studious ones, tried to dissuade us from undertaking the 'stupid' venture. They had insisted that if we wanted to persist with our crazy venture, we should think of doing a solid fuel rocket, as it would be easier to fabricate. But, as usual, we had brushed aside their genuine concerns and said a solid fuel rocket was like a Diwali fireworks cracker. Hence, it was below our dignity to fabricate and fire such a cheap and rotten thing!

After months of planning, reading books in the college library, and drawing intricate designs in exercise books, we thought we were Mr. Goddard himself, and grandly finalized the design of our liquid fuel rocket. The last part of our venture was a clandestine raid on Mr. Boparai's aero-modelling club, to procure some balsa wood and nitro-methane fuel for the rocket engine, which we grandly presumed would send our rocket into space!

The engine was made of aluminum canisters that we had removed from the photo lab – it was the cover of Kodak film rolls. The firing mechanism was a matchbox which Unni had pick pocketed from Thople, the rotund butler. Finally, the time came to test our rocket motor, before the projectile was formally launched. We had solemnly carried our rocket motor to an isolated spot near the tennis courts, to test its combustion chamber. At the test site, we filled liquid fuel in the rocket's fuel tank. As all our preparations were complete, our gang took up its positions, to watch the test and applaud. Manu Dutt was commissioned as an official photographer, and given my box camera to take photographs and record the event for posterity! Since Unni was the chief instigator and the designer of the propulsion unit, he was elected to fire and evaluate the engine performance and the thrust that it achieved – whether it was capable of reaching the Troposphere!

Since all mischief, in general, was instigated and supervised by me, I will call myself the self-styled Spacecraft Launch Director. As the scheduled time approached, the rocket engine (aluminium film-roll canisters), was fuelled with the very pungent nitro-methane and Unni ceremonially struck up a match-stick.

I loudly began the count-down, *'10-9- 8- 7- 6-5-4-3-2-1...FIRE!'*

The bystanders had all readied their hands to clap when Unni touched the lighted match to the well-fuelled combustion chamber. There was suddenly a big bang, as the combustion chamber exploded! Our months of careful preparations literally went up in flames! The spectators forgot about the well intended applause and ran helter-skelter to safety. Manu Dutt was surely not one to be left behind; he forgot about taking any photos and ran off with my box camera. The explosion sprayed some burning fuel on Unni's legs that were naked below his PT shorts, and the hair on his legs went up in flames. Unni lunged aside with a massive leap and sprinted madly from the hallowed rocket test-site, swatting his bottom and legs, alternately, to put out the fire. After the rocket test had ended quite unceremoniously, we dejectedly trooped back to our dormitory. On the way, I heard gay laughter because of poor Unni's fate. Both his legs were charred black below the knees, and the flames had left the legs scarred at many places and singed the hair on his legs.

Sitting on the dormitory's steps, after being challenged by studious cadets preparing for the ISC exam, I repeated, '*Let's do something spectacular and leave a mark.*'

Reluctantly, the others nodded their heads and asked almost in unison, '*Do what?*'

That was the time the very industrious Unni came up with a brilliant suggestion, '*Let's dig an underground room, where we can hide our tuck and other precious things.*'

'*That is a very good idea,*' said Fatty.

'*It will surely leave a mark, but where the hell should we dig it?*' I had asked softly.

After debating heatedly, we not only selected the site for our venture but also agreed on a design and a plan of action to get it done. We christened our project as the 'Shoe', because of its proposed shape. The selected site was close to our dormitory, in a hidden location and overall it was relatively secure. The site was located in tall hedgerows behind Ranjit Section Senior Dormitory and on one side of the road leading to Mr. K Kumar's house. We remembered this as a secure location, as we had used it earlier to cook up 'witch's brew' and for many other nefarious activities. For this operation, we did an engineering assessment as well as a work-study one and realised that we would require enormous manpower for the digging, as also to spread the soil around in a manner that our venture was we were not discovered. So we decided to rope in practically all our friends, each with a specific task. Fatty and Kajla were to procure the digging implements surreptitiously. Tota, Soli, and Tinda were to help spread the mud! They were to make holes in their pockets, fill their pockets with mud and go for walks all along the track from Ranjit Section to the mandir, spreading the mud so no one would suspect that we had been digging the 'Shoe'. HS Vaid, the 'giraffe', was to stand as a watch tower and warn us of any approaching threat, by making sounds like the confounded owl that used to inquisitively follow us during our night-time mischievous adventures!

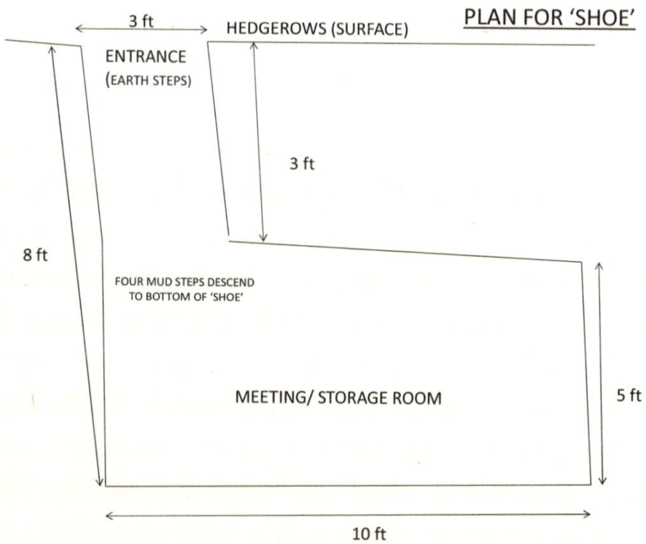

Our next hurdle was to procure a pair of garden shears, *khurpi*, pick-axes, and shovels. This problem was solved by Fatty and Kajla, who struck up a friendly conversation about birds, bees, flowers, and trees, with the gardener. While his back was turned, Unni and Tinda silently made off with the required tools. Later the gardener complained to Subedar Limbu, our drill and PT staff.

When we were questioned, we had appeared shocked and feigned complete innocence, *'Limbu Shab, ham kaishe aisha kar sakta hai ?'*

We commiserated in a Nepali accent that usually infuriated Sub Limbu. *'Tum sala lok, very badmash hai. Ham AO shaab ko complaint karega,'* he threatened and waved his stick at us.

However, we could not fool old Bhim Singh, the school's head *mali*, who knew we were involved in some mischievous activity, but he did not know what exactly we were up to! We kept the tools hidden in the cooler for a day. After dinner, the next day, we solemnly gathered at the site to begin our dream project. With the garden sheers we neatly cut a small hollow in the large, thorny, hedgerow and enlarged it internally like an igloo, so that the entrance of 'Shoe' would remain securely hidden from all curious passers-by. Precisely at the centre of the igloo we began to dig the 'Shoe'. On the first night, we were indeed very enthusiastic and dug rapidly in shifts. All around us there was a smell of freshly dug earth and by midnight we were tired, and lay down to rest.

We had gone down about four feet and it was becoming difficult to bring up the dug earth to the surface. Once the dug-earth was on top, the spreaders'took over and spread the mud all the way to the *mochi* shop and mandir. However, we knew this was only a temporary solution and we would very soon have to find a better method of earth disposal, if we didn't want to be caught out by Bhim Singh and his team of *malis*. After dinner on the next day, when we went to the 'Shoe' to dig, we were full of good spirits and humour. We found another hollow beneath the hedgerow into which we could safely fill with earth that we dug from the 'Shoe', where it would not be noticed. To our great glee, we found that some bandicoots were helping us to dig after we left and had gone to bed! Our digging work proceeded at top speed and within a week, we had prepared the basic hideout. Since it was dark within the 'Shoe', the resourceful Fatty magically produced a stub of candle. However, we decided to light the candle only during times of an emergency, and that too not more than two minutes at a stretch, because we had realised that depletion of oxygen in the 'Shoe' was leading to breathlessness and nausea.

One night, while we were digging underground inside the 'Shoe', Paltu[2] (a bearer in Pratap Section Middle Dorm) who was going home to the servant's quarters of Mr. K Kumar's house, heard us laughing loudly in the 'Shoe'. He got off his bicycle and inquisitively begun to peep under the hedgerows. Apparently, Giraffe (Vaid) had failed to give us a warning, or probably his owl calls had sounded funny like mating calls of peacocks! We realised that Paltu would become a dire threat to our project. So Fatty had acted instantly. He jumped out of the hedge and loudly yelled *'Boooo!!'* [3].

A very scared Paltu promptly ran away and mounted his cycle. He had pedaled furiously to Mr. K Kumar's house, like the proverbial bat out of hell! The next day Paltu had told everyone in Pratap Middle Dorm, there were some terrible ghosts in the hedges behind Ranjit Senior Dorm and cadets should be very careful on dark nights.

'*How will we know we've seen a ghost?*' The cadets of Pratap Middle Dorm had asked Paltu incredulously.

'*Well, ghosts laugh loudly when they see humans,*' he had said confidently.

'*If you go too close, they loudly say BOOOO, to warn you to run away and disappear,*' Paltu had continued very seriously.

So, some cadets from Pratap Section may have grown thinking there were ghosts behind Ranjit Section Senior Dormitory! It took us about 10 days to complete digging the 'Shoe'. We then nicely camouflaged the entrance in the hedgerow, to prevent other prying Paltu's from finding our prized hideout.

During one of our raids on the canteen, we managed to procure a large tin filled with Lacto Bon Bon sweets. The tin was hefted underground and hidden in the 'Shoe'. In the morning when we left for Doon School to take the ISC exams, each cadet from Ranjit Section was given a couple of sweets from the large Lacto Bon Bon tin, for good luck. It is another matter that instead of using the Bon Bons to bring luck in the exams, Unni went and offered his share of Bon Bons to a pretty girl from Welhams School, who sat in the adjacent row of seats. Though she willingly took the sweets, the girl paid scant attention to Unni [4]. During our adventure-filled days and right in the middle of the exams, Unni was besotted by this girl named Sita Ramaswami, who sat alongside him in the exam hall, in Doon School. He desperately wanted to reach out and talk to her. So, when we got back after our ISC exam paper, we collected in the 'Shoe' to resolve this very important and earth-shaking problem. After a long discussion, it was decided that we would write her a love letter on behalf of Unni and he would only have to give her the letter. After a lot of thinking and scratching our heads, with both good and crazy inputs from all 'Shoe-makers', we drafted a love letter. It was a first-time experience for us all. That night, we violated our self-imposed restriction of not keeping the candle burning for more than a few minutes. It took us nearly an hour to compose the quarter page long, flowery, and a ridiculous-sounding love note. By the time we emerged from the 'Shoe', we were all coughing badly and suffered from mild nausea and awful headaches. Today, I frankly think the headaches and nausea had nothing to do with the lit candle. It was caused by the most unusual mental exertions we had been through while composing and writing that ridiculous love letter!

Next morning we were very excited and reached Doon School a little early. The examination hall was empty and there was a blank answer booklet placed on all the examination tables. We looked on as Unni carefully placed the letter within pages of the blank answer booklet placed on the girl's table. Later, we got busy with the examination and seriously tackled the mathematics paper – for which we had hardly studied! After the examination, without any expression on her face, Sita Ramaswami pocketed the letter and marched out of the hall with her friends. Unni kept on looking at her walk away, without even giving him a nod. Poor Unni looked like a squirrel that had lost his nuts! We forcibly pulled him into our one-ton truck and returned to RIMC. Back in school we hardly prepared for our last examination that was scheduled the next day – the English paper. We tried our best to lift Unni's sagging spirits, by telling him stupid stories of the chaos we would create during the coming holidays but, we were quite unsuccessful in our attempts and Unni remained as sullen, as ever. The next morning, we trooped into the exam hall and were handed our English question paper. I had just started writing in my answer booklet when I heard some unusual, sputtering sounds from behind me. On turning back, I saw my friend Unni, looking very pale as if he had seen a ghost. He was sitting at an unusual angle and reading a small piece of paper he had discovered in his answer booklet. Apparently, the girl had done the same thing as our friend – she had arrived early at the hall and slipped a reply into our friend's answer booklet! The reply simply said '*Hi, thanks for the Bon Bons. Bye.*'

The loud, sputtering sounds were coming from Unni,

who in his great excitement on seeing the 'Hi and Bye' note, was trying to laugh and cry at the very same time!

That was a great beginning and rapid end of the first Bon Bon love affair of our peer group! Later, nearly all of us had similar Bon Bon experiences, when our respective turns came to fall in love. The unusual fact was that even after the monumental distractions of love and no love, we all (including Unni) passed in the ISC Exam, even though we had not touched a book and did not belong to the studious category. Unni surprised us all and actually did quite well. Nearly every day we would go to the hedgerow and descend into the hidden entrance of our 'Shoe'. We would climb down over the four steps we had cut in the earth and get to the bottom of 'Shoe'. Once we were at the bottom, we would feel safe and secure sitting about eight feet below the surface. In the darkened space, we would seriously discuss various important topics, such as Overall Section Championships, the menu at the mess, pictures (movies) running at theatres in town, etc. We neither had the time nor inclination to discuss about other cadets, our teachers, staff, or any such-like irrelevant issues. Sometimes, of course, we would discuss the benefits and hazards of dating or befriending girls like Sita Ramaswami. Unni would argue eloquently against the motion, and harp on the issue that for future soldiers, love was not to be! However, once we were past nineteen, I think Unni Kartha fell in love with every girl he happened to see!

Looking back many years later, I find it really amazing how the roof of 'Shoe' held out and did not collapse on us, fifteen-year-olds! With a juvenile lack of knowledge, we had neither erected props and nor did we have any supports to hold up the roof of heavy, earth. It was an engineers' nightmare and a ready-made coffin just waiting for a disaster to occur! Many years later, as Commander of a Brigade during Kargil operations, I was briefing Chief of Army Staff (COAS), when in-coming enemy shells began to hit our command post of reinforced concrete. A section of the roof collapsed and I suddenly remembered the ruddy 'Shoe'. I think I said '*Shoe is safe,*' right in the middle of the briefing. The COAS and others present must have thought that I had crossed the thin red line and gone crazy with the stress!

In 2010, I went to school for the *Rimcollians* reunion for the first time since we had passed out in 1966! During the reunion, Unni and I went behind Ranjit Senior Dormitory to expectantly look for 'Shoe'. We stood at the place where the igloo and entrance had been located. There was a small depression in the ground, but no 'Shoe'! We sat there for a while and looked around us. Old memories came flooding back. Ranjit Section Senior Dormitory was in its old place, so was the mess, the college office, and parade ground. Old Mr. K Kumar's house could be seen at the end of the road. Near the college office, we could see some *malis* working on beds of colourful flowers. The gardens were surely looking better and they were more colourful than they had been in our time. Our gaze returned to the small depression in the ground. It was nearly a flat piece of ground now, and there were no hedgerows or even a bush.

Though today Fatty has disappeared from the horizon, like so many others, I said softly and sadly, '*Fatty, old chap, we finally did not leave a mark as we had planned! The ruddy 'Shoe' itself has disappeared.*'

Sitting at RIMC in 2010 as senior citizens, Unni and I decided that during our next visit, we would plant a sapling of the red-silk-cotton tree (*simbal* tree) with a mysterious plaque marking the location of 'The Shoe'[13].

Although many winters having passed (as Mr. S Bandopadhya, our one-time English teacher, would often say), we have remained as incorrigible as ever. On 13 March 2010, we had laughed happily at the thought that some perplexed cadets would one day read the writing on the mysterious plaque and wonder what 'The Shoe' really meant! We had even reverently hoped that some future cadets would launch a flurry of juicy rumours that would drape a cloak of great secrecy and mystery around 'The Shoe'. One day, a mighty *simbal* tree will tower over the countryside and mark the location of 'The Shoe'. It would herald the tremendous spirit of adventure that lives in the minds of cadets of RIMC. The mighty tree would highlight that our towering thoughts, while sitting on Ranjit Section Senior Dormitory steps on the lazy Sunday morning in early 1966, has come true and we did manage to leave a mark, of sorts! Boys of RIMC never really grow up, and happily, the spirit of adventure and mischief lives on, even after many winters have passed.

---

13 *The red-silk-cotton tree was duly planted in 2011, and will hopefully one day tower over the RIMC campus.*

[1] 'Fatty' Daljit Singh Grewal was not really a fat boy. He was actually a lean, tall, gifted sportsman and an extremely energetic fellow; the most mischievous amongst us. Many of the sobriquets that boys invented for each other in their peer group had nothing to do with anything real (like Tanga, Mamu, Tota, Tinda, etc.), except in some cases like Lambu, Hook Nose, etc. that had something to do with appearance – these names were given in fun, and mostly stayed for life !!!

[2] After we left RIMC for NDA in 1966, Paltu was promoted to the rank of a mess waiter.

[3] The same technique had been successfully employed during 'Biscuit Raid', when one of the raiders suddenly found himself face to face with the Catering JCO, at the door of college's bakery store.

[4] Seating arrangements in the examination hall (at Doon School) was along adjacent rows, for Welhams Girls School, RIMC and Doon School respectively.

About the Author

Brigadier Jasbir Singh, SM, is a *Rimcollian* who studied in RIMC from mid-1962 to 1966. Thereafter, he did his training in NDA Kharavasla and IMA Dehradun, where he was commissioned in 4 Kumaon (*Fighting Fourth*). He was wounded during operations behind enemy lines in East Pakistan (1971 war) and twice decorated for gallantry during operations.

After having served for 34 years in the Army, he now leads a retired life in the hills of Ranikhet and spends his time writing on military subjects and painting. He is the author of nine books and numerous articles.

His father, Brigadier Balbir Singh, MC, was also from the Kumaon Regiment, and he escaped from a Japanese POW Camp in Singapore during World War II, an exploit detailed in his previous book *The POW Who Saved Kashmir*.

He is also the author of a vibrant history of his battalion—4 Kumaon—about to be published.